If I Am So Smart,
Why Can't I Lose Weight?

Tools To Get It Done

By Brooke Castillo

Author's Note

Throughout this book I have used examples from many of my personal clients' lives. However, to ensure privacy and confidentiality I have changed some of their names and some of the details of their experience. All of the personal examples of my own life have not been altered.

Second Printing, 2007

ISBN-13: 978-1-4196-1847-5

Library of Congress Number: 2005909622

Page Design: Janice M. Phelps

Cover Design: Cathi Stevenson

To order additional copies, please contact us.
BookSurge, LLC
www.booksurge.com
1-866-308-6235
orders@booksurge.com
www.FuturesUnlimitedCoaching.com

To Martha
For telling me to go big.

Notice

This book contains discussions about health issues and medical problems. While I have my own opinions about these subjects, they are just opinions based on my skill, training, and knowledge. I am not a physician; if you should have questions about a medical problem, please refer to your primary-care physician or a medical consultant. In addition, please be advised that I cannot be held responsible for medical decisions you make as a result of reading this book. Please contact your physician before undertaking any of the recommendations I may make.

Table of Contents

Acknowledgments

To pick up and read another book on weight loss is a testament to your undying faith and your belief in the existence of an answer to the weight problem. Considering the amount of information out there and the piles of stuff that just hasn't worked, I applaud your spirit for giving it another try. I hope you keep going and keep trying things until you find your answer—until you find what works for you. I hope you find it here.

To my husband, Chris, I have always said I won the husband lottery—and I know I did. You made this book possible by taking the kids to school, helping them with their homework, and telling them to be quiet when Mom was working. You make my life a +10. I love you.

To my boys who were quiet when I was typing and who understood that what I was doing was important; also, for not touching the delete key on the keyboard even when it was sooooo tempting; for reminding me that food could never be better than a friend at the door who wants to play; and for showing me that it is possible to eat one fourth of a peanut butter sandwich and throw the rest away because you're "full." You are my teachers each and every day.

To Suyin for believing in me and herself enough to be my very first success story. You are an inspiration to many clients who came after you.

To my mom for always being my biggest fan and telling me that I could do anything I wanted to do with my life. I am so glad I believed you.

To Marik, Kirk, Erika, Penny, Lorie, Matt M., Dennis, and Wendy for encouraging me, supporting me, and allowing me to test all my tools on you. Without you, I wouldn't be a coach.

To Allison Brown for walking me so kindly through this book publishing process. To Arielle Ford for her encouraging feedback and great publishing advice. And to Janice Phelps and Joan Phelps for all your help in presenting the interior and editing. I am so appreciative to you all.

Finally—to my clients. You have all put up with me getting excited over your negative emotions and screaming with glee when you had a negative situation to face. Your successes fuel me and show me that it's all worth it. Your courage to go for it and your willingness to learn inspires me everyday. Each one of you has made my life better. Rock on girls! Get it done!

Introduction

A weight loss coach? That is something I haven't tried yet, and I thought I had tried everything." This is usually the response I get after someone asks me what I do for a living. Then, they want to know about the diet I give my clients and what I have them do to work out. Many ask what kind of supplements I sell or if I provide packaged meals. Many people have never heard of a life coach, let alone a life coach who specializes specifically on weight loss. They have no idea what I can offer if it isn't a diet.

I don't offer a diet, pre-packaged meals, or a magic pill. This book is not about me telling you what to do. It is not about me telling you what I eat specifically every day so you can do the same. My work and this book are about you finding *your* answers. It is based on the belief that you have your own wisdom with the exact formula of what works. Even though I think this is amazing news, which is empowering and exciting, many of my clients do not. They don't want to "go in," they want me to give them structure, rules, and limits. They feel out of control and want to be managed.

I always disappoint in this way. No matter how many times they ask for structure, I give them challenging emotional assignments designed to bring up their emotions and obstacles so they can get to know themselves. I never give them an external cure for the extra fat they carry on their bodies. I see the fat as a message to go in and find out what is going on emotionally. I see it as an opportunity to begin some important work in their life.

One of my clients put it this way: "If I had known where this process would take me, I would not have ever signed up. That would have been the biggest mistake of my life. Not only have I lost weight, but I have found joy in my life again."

The weight is the signal to go in and solve the under-lying problem. It is the physical manifestation of an internal issue. This process takes you into those issues and helps you change them because they are the cause of the weight. I don't spend too much time working on treating the symptom, because once you solve the underlying issue, the symptom will slowly disappear.

I have written this book in a way that will take you through the process I use with my clients. In the first sessions we will work on eating and the "relearning" of how to connect to your physical body. I will give you many tools to understand your body and its sensations of hunger and how to eat in a way where you never feel deprived. Once you start feeling more connected to your body and your wisdom, we focus on exercise as another way to connect to your physical body, but also as a way to build your mental strength and com mitment to yourself.

As you get more solidly connected with your physical self, you will start being more truly connected emo-tionally. Feelings will start to bubble up and emotions start surfacing. This is exactly what we want to have happen. I push you to create more situations that intensify the process and set you up for exposure to all the negative feelings and beliefs you are carrying. This might not sound like any fun, but it is necessary to get into your emotional life. I teach you each tool to use in handling your emotional life in a healthy and life-changing way. As you apply the tools to your life, it becomes more manageable and you become more joyful, connected, and free. The tools help you reach inside and find your true self, hiding under the struggle.

You will start to discover things besides your weight struggles—like desires, dreams, and goals. We unfold these and honor them. We listen to your heart. Then, I'll teach you more tools to start pursuing ways in which you will find true joy. As we make action plans to move you into a more joyful life, you will use the emotional tools you had been practicing. You will remember that there is nothing you can't do if you really want it...including losing weight.

Feel free to read straight through the book one time so you can have a general idea of how all the tools work together and how the whole process will work. Then go back to the beginning and start doing the exercises and applying the knowledge to your life. Understanding these tools intellectually will make you smarter. Applying them in your life will make you thin. It really doesn't matter how much you know or understand.

Until you apply it, by taking action, it has very little value in your life.

Learn the tool, apply it, and practice it, then learn another. Apply each tool as soon as possible after learning it so you can start to make it a habit in your life. It may feel awkward at first because it's new, but after some consistent application and practice it will begin to feel natural. When you have completed this book, your tool belt will be full. With your true self and a few tools, there is nothing you can't handle.

This book answers the question on the front cover: Why can't I lose weight? Then, it gives you the tools to use *your* smarts in order to lose weight for good. I am not a doctor, a personal trainer, a therapist, or a nutritionist. I have borrowed from all these professions in developing this coaching practice, but I do not pretend to have their schooling or smarts.

In fact, I have coached many clients in these professions who are very smart, but they have not been able to lose the weight. Sometimes, too much knowledge and being too smart intellectually can blind you from the internal wisdom and your inner guide. In these cases, we need to forget what we know intellectually and remember what we know intuitively.

I have personally studied weight loss materials my whole life. I have been on every diet and tried almost every gimmick. It wasn't until I learned how to believe in myself and love myself by using the tools outlined in this book that I ended the struggle with my weight. Today, I am seventy pounds lighter than I was at my heaviest. I have ended the battle with myself and my weight forever. I now use the energy that I had turned against myself in my coaching practice.

There is no doubt in my mind that you can end your struggle too. I have seen client after client, who had turned on themselves, redirect that energy and make many of their dreams come true.

If we can do it, you can do it.

Let's go get it done.

Eating Is Not
Rocket Science

*"No diet can substitute for the
wisdom of your own body."*

Eating Tool #1
Your Brilliant Body

Eating. Yes, eating has been the hardest part of every attempt to lose weight. Eating the right foods in the right amounts and at the right times based on the diet you are following can be very tedious. Eating becomes confusing and difficult when we have many external rules to follow and we aren't following the wisdom of our own bodies. We have been sold a bill of goods about why we are overweight. Every new diet sells us a new reason why we can't lose weight and how, for a small price, their diet is the answer. My suggestion is for you to forget every food combination fad scam you have ever heard and just remember the truth.

The reason you are overweight is because:

YOU EAT MORE THAN YOUR BODY REQUIRES FOR FUEL.

Period.

End of story.

I know this seems basic, but it is amazing how easily we forget the basics. We start believing the sales pitch for the diet products and stop believing the truth. There are two parts to this basic truth that we need to evaluate. The first part is that you eat more than is required.

There are two reasons why people overeat and both reasons include ignoring your body:

The first reason people overeat is due to too much deprivation. They restrict their food intake for a period of time by going on a crash diet or trying not to eat at all. Inevitably, they end up overeating because for each unrealistic restriction there is an equal and opposite "overeat." By going on a highly restrictive diet you must disconnect from your body's signals of hunger and feed it according to some external plan. This is painful for both you and your body. Once the disconnection has been maintained for a certain amount of time, the urge to eat becomes unbearable for your body, whose job it is to keep you from starving. You end up eating much more than you need. The disconnection from your body has now exacerbated this issue because the denial of the hunger signal now leads to denial of the full signal and the overeating is rampant. This is why you end up eating much more than you normally did before you went on the diet.

> *Your body is primal.*
> *It thinks you live in a cave*
> *with limited food available.*

When we don't honor our hunger and eat according to our body, we create problems with our metabolism. When we deprive the body of food, it's designed to slow down, conserve energy, and *hold on to fat*. It does this to protect us and to keep us alive when there is little food available. It's a brilliant design. When we were cave dwellers, our body needed to adjust between times of feast and times of famine. When there was no food available, our cave-dwelling body adjusted its metabolic rate, the rate at which it used up food. Our metabolic rate went down and we hung on to every calorie we got to use and store nutrition for later. Fortunately, we aren't cave dwellers any more and we have plenty of food to eat (and we don't use up the calories trying to catch it). For example, when we choose to strictly diet and eat very little food, our body turns into a cave dweller and adjusts our metabolic rate downward. We hold on to every calorie. When we keep our bodies reasonably fed, they know that there is no need to keep extra fat around because there is plenty of food coming at regular intervals. Your metabolism speeds up and the fat comes off.

On a smaller scale, you may not eat all day until your body starts screaming (then you'll listen). By that time, your body is starting to wonder if there is any food available and goes into "you-must-eat-immediately" mode. At this point, you eat past satiation just to get your body to calm down. Either way, you end up overeating because your body is trying to protect you and take care of you.

The second reason people overeat is a lack of awareness and complete disconnection. Many people in America are unconscious eaters; they just check out and eat without awareness all the time. They are completely out of touch with their body and are not conscious of what its needs are; therefore, they just eat all day long with no regard to hunger and with no regard to nutritional value. They eat based on what is available, on timing, and on circumstances.

This type of eating reasons that it is morning and time

> *Paying attention to what you eat is a huge part of staying consciously awake for your life.*

to eat whether the body is hungry or not. So you eat, but how do you know when to stop eating? You weren't hungry when you started so how will you know when you are full? Many times you overeat. Then it is time to go to work and there is a plate of food for everyone to share again; you eat some to be social with no regard for your body. Then, it's time for lunch. You certainly aren't hungry because you ate so much already, but it's lunch time (time to eat again) and you are at a restaurant with some clients, so you order a meal and eat it all, your body and its opinion being completely irrelevant.

If too much deprivation leads to overeating and being disconnected leads to overeating, the answer becomes eating only what our body requires for fuel. So how do we know how much our body requires for fuel? Many of us think we need to go see a nutritionist and ask them to give us a formula based on how much time we spend doing certain activities and how many calories

> *Eat only what your body requires for fuel.*

we expend. Then, we believe we will be able to determine exactly how many calories we need to eat. Then, all we have to do is count each one that goes into our mouth and make sure we stay at the number the nutritionist provided. There are many experts who will give us very complicated and scientific formulas to follow and labels to read. But even the sophisticated science is not exactly customized to *your* body.

I have a much easier suggestion. If you really think about it, the true expert of how much your body requires for fuel is your body. If you want to know how much your body requires for fuel, ask it. It comes (at no extra charge to you) with a sophisticated communication device. It's called hunger and fullness. It whispers to you daily, all day long. It takes practice to pay attention and honor its signals. It requires you to stay in the present moment and connect to yourself. If you will listen to your hunger and fullness, your body will give you the exact formula for eating. If you follow it, you will only eat exactly what you need. It really is as simple as that. The expert is built in and has been with you this entire time; you have just been ignoring it!

The choice has been to pay attention to your beautiful, brilliant, complex body that whispers wisdom to you all day long, or to turn your attention outward and pay attention to the money-making organizations that want you to listen to them. Restaurants with huge portions want you to come in and order appetizers, dinner, and desserts. Fast food wants you to ignore your body long enough so you will be so hungry, you will drive through and super size a meal to get rid of your screaming hunger. The diet industry wants to teach you how to ignore your body so you will keep failing and keep coming back for more. It sickens me to think I sold my body out for so many years.

Think about how much you have underutilized the most amazing tool you have. Your body is a brilliant source of wisdom. It runs the most complicated organization of processes that you can't begin to understand. It truly has wisdom beyond our wildest comprehen-

---

Pay attention to your beautiful, brilliant, complex body's wisdom.

sion. Yet, we ignore it and call 1-800-STARVEME instead. Trust your body to tell you how to feed it. It's the expert on what you should be eating. It knows your body better than any diet, expert, or calculation. It knows what food makes it feel good. It knows when it wants to eat. It knows when it's satisfied. You have been trained to ignore your body by eating too much, then depriving it later by going on a diet. You need to retrain yourself to pay attention to your body and its wisdom. If you will listen to what it says about eating, it will listen to what you have to say about releasing some fat.

Eating Tool #2
The Hunger Scale

Since you have picked up this book, I will make the assumption that you are not in tune with your body. I will assume that when I say eat when you're hungry and stop when you're full, you have questions. So, I have designed a tool that will help you get back in touch with your body and what it is trying to communicate to you. It's called the hunger scale and it's just like the fuel tank in your car, except that it's the fuel tank for your body.

The first step in using the hunger scale is to make sure you know what hunger feels like. I am not talking about the crazy, starving hunger that screams at you when you have gone many hours without eating. I am talking about the whisper that you will need to listen to to really hear your body's wisdom. This whisper is faint and subtle and is often ignored. We're going to break it down so there is no mistake when you are actually feeling it.

The first distinction that needs to be made is the difference between the sensation of hunger and feeling hunger. The sensation of hunger is a biological and physical reaction caused by the lack of fuel. You will need to spend a lot of time getting to know what this really feels like. It's a connection to your body that tells you on a physical level where you are on the hunger scale. An emotional feeling of hunger can be very similar, but it's harder to locate in the body. Many times, emotional hunger is felt more in the chest and the heart. It's not accompanied by a sense of lightness or emptiness, but more of a heavy emptiness. It's heavy and dull. You will have your own distinctions, but you must learn the difference. When you want to honor a hunger signal and listen to your hunger emotion, you need to know the difference so you can treat each one with the proper tools and actions. Too often we are eating from emotional hunger and filling our stomach when we need to be filling our hearts.

The following exercise is a clear way to understand the difference within your body. You will make a list of what it feels like when you are physically hungry for food and what that feels like in your body. On the other side of the page, you need to write down what your emotional hunger feels like. Take a first pass at this now. As you continue on this journey and start paying more attention, you will really be able to refine the list so there will be no question of what the difference is. I have given you some examples to get you started, but feel free to change and customize them to exactly match your own body and experience.

> *The sensation of hunger*
> *is satisfied with fuel;*
> *the emotion of hunger*
> *is satisfied with self-love.*

Sensations vs. Feelings Worksheet

Describe the physical sensation of hunger below:	Describe the emotional needs/feelings that might make you feel hungry or the need to eat below:
1. *(Example: My stomach feels empty and makes noises.)*	1. <u>Anger:</u> *I want to use food to stuff down my fury.*
2. *(Example: My mouth gets wet.)*	2. <u>Loneliness:</u> *I am comforted by warm, yummy food when alone.*
3. *(Example: My body feels weak.)*	3. <u>Happiness:</u> *I enjoy food when I am with my friends.*
4. *(Example: My brain actively seeks options for eating.)*	4. <u>Boredom:</u> *I am looking for food to entertain me, so I don't have to entertain myself.*
5.	5.

Sensations vs. Feelings Worksheet

6.   6.

7.   7.

8.   8.

9.   9.

10.   10.

Physical Hunger Scale

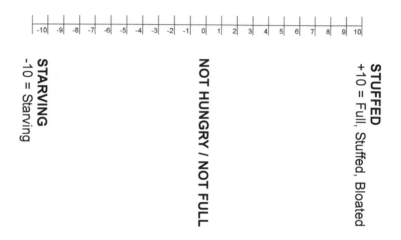

Hunger Scale

This is the hunger scale used for physical hunger only. It runs from -10, which is starving, to +10, which is stuffed. Zero is neutral where you are not hungry and you are not full. You need to use this scale as a gauge, like the fuel gauge in your car. When your body gets to -2, it's time to feed it. When you get to +2, you stop eating. This will keep you in a range where you will never really get too hungry and you will never feel deprived. You will feel satisfied, yet light, all day long. Your body will know that it's going to be fed regularly according to its needs.

If you can learn this one tool and actually be willing to apply it, you will solve your weight issue. It is the most challenging practice because when you stop at 2, your feelings and beliefs will surface and feel very uncomfortable at first. You will learn throughout this book how to use these feelings and beliefs to make your life richer, but for now you must understand the simple truth: STOPPING AT 2 ON A REGULAR BASIS IS THE FIRST INDICATION YOU ARE TRULY CONNECTED TO YOURSELF AND YOUR BODY.

If you look at the scale, you can see that it is a very small range right in the middle that I am suggesting you stay within. It is about the size of your stomach (which is about the size of your fist). As you get to know your -2, you will realize that it is just a little whisper from your body that it is time for a little fuel.

EATING -2 to 2 on
the hunger scale
consistently will take
your body to its
natural weight.

It doesn't scream or interrupt you with a loud growl. It is a very subtle emptiness with a little gentle growl. You need to be in the present moment and connected to hear it. At this point, you have enough time to prepare a small meal or snack and eat.

As you are eating, you will slowly notice your body moving from -2, to -1, to 0. Then, you will feel your stomach filling up and moving to 1, then 2. As you arrive at 2, you will need to stop eating. This means that if you are right in the middle of a meal, a sandwich, or a protein shake—stop. In the beginning, I suggest being hyper-vigilant here. This is very important in terms of retraining your body that you trust it and that you are listening. This is not a time for justifications or rationalizations. Do not judge your body for its opinion. Just get to know it.

Many times, my clients are shocked by how quickly they get to 2. For some, it takes very little food. It is amazing for them to eat so little and not feel physical deprivation. By the very definition of being at 2 on the hunger scale, you will feel satiation and not physical deprivation. Other times, diet flashbacks and worry will come up. Just let those feelings surface and remember that you are truly physically satiated at this point.

As you might have guessed, by eating according to your body and its wisdom, you will be eating more often throughout the day. This usually requires some planning to have food with you and available so you won't go beyond –2. You will feel comfortable stopping at 2, knowing you have more food available for the very next time you get hungry.

It is okay to play around with the food scale and eat only a few bites to get you to -1 to hold you over for an upcoming dinner or a planned event. Be careful to not let yourself ever get too hungry. Keep yourself fed before you get past -2 so you won't be in such a hurry to eat everything in sight. When you get too hungry, you set yourself up to eat convenient foods and not necessarily what your body needs. Stop eating at 2 so you can feel light and not feed your body more than it needs.

Never let your body get below -2 on the hunger scale.

> *Listening to your body and honoring its signals is one of the true forms of self-love.*

This is a practice and a way of life. It requires you to invest your time and energy into your relationship with your body. It requires you to respect it. It requires you to listen to it. In the middle of a meal at a restaurant, you will need to connect to yourself and listen. For many of us, it is not in our programming to stay connected, so it will take some effort at first. If you really work at it, eventually you will get used to having a light feeling in your stomach and an intimate communication with your body. It becomes a natural way of being in your own skin. You get to the point where overeating is akin to shoving more food in the mouth of a child who has said he has had enough. You start listening to your body with the same respect you would give that child. By gently laying your fork down, you are telling your body you are listening.

Naturally thin people who have not been subjected to diets do this without thinking. If you watch thin people eat, you will notice that they don't order large quantities of food and they regularly stop when they have had enough. They may stop in the middle of a meal or lose interest halfway through a dessert. To many of us this is astounding. We cannot imagine stopping in the middle of a dish that tastes so good. To a naturally thin person, it does not make sense to continue feeding a body that isn't hungry. To them, it would be like overfilling the gas tank of a car. Even if it is the highest grade gasoline and the price is ridiculously low, there is still no reason to fill a tank past full. It doesn't take effort or forethought; it seems incredibly obvious to stop when full.

You and your body are on the same side. You need to keep it that way if you want your body to cooperate, and you can work together to achieve your goals. As long as you are fighting against your body, you will be in a fight that will never end.

> *You and your body*
> *are on the same side.*

Exercise:

- On a sheet of paper write a diagram of the hunger scale.

- Next to each of the numbers write a description of how your body feels at each number.

- As you go through this program, try to get even more specific. Really get to know yourself and your body. For example, at -2, I feel slightly lightheaded and there is a gentle growl in my stomach. At -1, I feel slightly empty, but the growl is gone and the lightheadedness is gone. At 0, I feel like I am about half-way full, but still want some more nourishment to keep me energized. At 1, I feel like I am getting energized and at 2 I feel light and satiated...ready to go. Now write down your feelings and description. This is so important to write down! Please do not just read this information and understand it. If you were my client, you would be required to write it down and apply it because it does you no good just floating around as an idea in your head. You must be able to apply it.

Structure based on the hunger scale

Many clients come to me and feel completely out of control. In order to get started, they want me to give them some structure that will automatically get them in touch with their hunger cues and learning the hunger scale. What I have found time and time again is that the body gets hungry for a small meal about every two to three hours. If you deliberately eat this way, you will start to notice that, when you eat small meals at an interval of about three hours, your stomach will be at -2 again. For those of you who want a little more structure getting started, here are some guidelines that should get you back in touch with your body. Remember, these are not guidelines you follow without regard to your body. If you find your body has a different plan, your body wins! But this should help you get started.

- Eat six small meals a day about every three hours (two of these meals can be a high-grade nutrition bar or protein shake).
- Eat a serving of fuel carbohydrates and a serving of fuel protein at each meal (more information on fuel foods later).
- Make sure at least 3 of the meals have a serving of vegetables.
- A serving size is the size of your fist (this is the actual size of your stomach).
- Drink an 8 oz. bottle of water every two hours.

I have found that this eating pattern automatically has most people eating when they are hungry and stopping at just about a 2 on the hunger scale. When you eat small meals all day long you stay within the range, never getting too hungry and never getting too full.

Not everyone needs to follow this type of structure, but it's a very good guideline for my clients who don't eat enough. This is how I eat and I have found that it delivers me a steady stream of energy throughout the day, keeps me within the range on the hunger scale, and is in line with my body's wisdom.

Eating Tool #3
The Four Types of Eating

Once you have a clear understanding of the hunger scale and you start to apply it, you will notice that there are many times when you are not hungry and you still want to eat. It may be when you are in the middle of a meal and you have reached 2, but you want to keep eating. Or, it might be in the middle of the day and you have no need for fuel, but you have a strong desire to eat something because it happens to be in front of you. Do not panic when this happens. In fact, this is not always a bad thing. If you are willing to pay attention to what is going on with your eating, you will have a window into your emotional life. Any time you want to eat for a non-fuel reason, you may have an opportunity to learn something. So, I recommend you look forward to this happening.

> *Anytime you want to eat food when you are not physically hungry is an opportunity to learn something.*

My clients have found it very helpful to categorize their eating so they can evaluate and understand when they are not eating according to their body's requirements for nourishment. Categorizing food also gives you a nice guideline of *what* to eat. Most times, you will want to eat fuel to energize your body, but sometimes, you will want to eat for the strict purpose of enjoyment. By separating these types of eating into categories, you can manage them and choose how much of each you want to do for your maximum emotional and physical health.

So the first thing we need to do is categorize our food into four different types. In this book I will refer to the four different types of eating as Fuel Eating, Joy Eating, Fog Eating and Storm Eating. Each time you eat you are in one of these four categories.

Fuel Eating

The reason we have to eat is to fuel our bodies. Fuel Eating is eating with awareness of nutrition and what makes your body energetic and well-functioning. Fuel foods are nutrient dense. Fuel foods include fruits, vegetables, lean proteins, complex carbohydrates, and healthy fats. A basic knowledge of nutrition is imperative for you to know what types of foods fuel your body and what ones do not. It is beyond the scope of my expertise to teach nutrition, but what I have found is that most of us know which foods fuel us by how they feel in our body. You can design what your healthy fuel menu looks like. It's not a strict set of guidelines. It's eating in a healthy way that feels good to you. If you still feel unsure, I highly recommend you pick up a copy of Bill Phillips' book *Eating for Life*. It will give you all the details of what constitutes a healthy meal without boring you with too many of the details. It is based on the six-meals-a-day eating principle, which flows well with the hunger scale of most bodies. It's a recipe book filled with small-course meals that are yummy and easy to prepare. I strongly recommend this book to all my clients and cook from it myself weekly.

There are many other very good eating plans you can use to help with your fuel eating. I have clients who have used *South Beach*, *Weight Watchers*, *Body for Life* and *e-diet* as guides to help them with fuel eating. They do not use dieting as their entire weight loss plan, but as a tool for fuel eating. I do not recommend using any diet to help with fuel eating that severely restricts calories or disconnects you from your body. Diets can be helpful in food choices, but your body will always tell you how much to eat. Ultimately, you need to decide what fuel works best for your body—not the external plan.

Fuel foods are like employees that have a job to do in your body. When you eat them, with the awareness of what they will do when they get into your body, you will see how they help you to function. For example, a healthy protein will provide the building blocks for cells; a complex carbohydrate will give you steady energy; a piece of fruit will give you essential nutrients and water; and vegetables are loaded with vitamins and minerals. High-grade foods, like high-quality employees, work hard for you. They go in and work to provide your body with the essentials it needs to function. Low-quality food that is over-processed with low-nutrient value is like hiring a lazy employee. Diet food or low-in-fat food that is designed to convince you that you are eating when there is no nutritional value, like hiring filler employees, is going to slow you down and cause you problems. Do a mini-interview with any food you put into your body. Hire and eat wisely!

Fuel eating should be done 90 percent of the time for maximum health. If you are filling your body on hunger cue with high-grade fuel, you will feel energized, healthy, and light most of the time. You will feel your metabolism kicking in from eating so often and feel each cell celebrating among vitamins and minerals. You really can't go wrong with your health if you are feeding yourself what you body needs to function optimally.

By the way, fuel food can taste amazing. Fuel food does not mean diet food in a freeze-dried container. Quite the opposite. A good fuel meal is fresh, simple, lean, and tastes great. I believe life is too short to eat anything that doesn't taste good. So, eat fuel foods you and your body both like.

The rules for fuel eating are:

- It must be something your body wants and needs.
- You must start at -2 and stop at +2 on the hunger scale.
- Fuel eat 90 percent of the time.

Two final notes on fuel eating:

1. As you begin to increase your exercise regime, you might think you need more fuel food to compensate. Do not make this mistake. Your body is always the one to indicate if you need extra fuel. Follow its cues and trust it.

2. Eating too much processed food and simple carbohydrates can alter the natural communication of the hunger scale. Any high-sugar foods that cause a spike followed by a dip in your blood sugar will send a false hunger signal and lead you to believe you are requiring more fuel when you aren't. Eating simple carbohydrates rarely and with a serving of protein will alleviate this issue.

Sample Fuel Food Choices

PROTEINS

Chicken Breast
Turkey Breast
Lean Ground Turkey
Orange Roughy
Haddock
Salmon
Tuna
Crab
Lobster
Shrimp
Top Round Steak
Top Sirloin Steak
Lean Ground Beef
Lean Ham
Egg Whites/Substitutes
Trout
Low-Fat Cottage Cheese
Wild Game Meat
Tofu
Soy Foods
Veggie Burgers

CARBOHYDRATES

Baked Potato
Sweet Potato
Yams
Squash
Steamed Brown Rice
Steamed Wild Rice
Pasta
Oatmeal
Barley
Beans
Kidney Beans
Corn
Strawberries
Melon
Apple
Orange
Fat-Free Yogurt
Whole-Grain Bread
High-Fiber Cereal
Whole-Wheat Tortilla
Whole Grains

Sample Fuel Food Choices

VEGETABLES

Broccoli
Asparagus
Lettuce
Carrots
Cauliflower
Green Beans
Green Peppers
Mushrooms
Spinach
Tomato
Peas
Brussel Sprouts
Artichokes
Cabbage
Celery
Zucchini
Cucumber
Onion

FATS

Avocado
Sunflower Seeds
Pumpkin Seeds
Cold-Water Fish
Natural Peanut Butter
Low-Fat Cottage Cheese
Low-Fat Salad Dressing
Low-Sodium Nuts
Olives and Olive Oil
Safflower Oil
Canola Oil
Sunflower Oil
Flax Seed Oil

Exercise:

- Make a list of all the fuel foods you like to eat. Jot down ideas on how you can prepare fuel food and have them available. List the fuel foods that you would like to add to your diet because they are good for you and they taste great. Note any changes you might have to make in order to plan to have fuel foods in your home and with you during your day.

FUEL FOODS THAT TASTE GOOD

(Example: Chicken Breast with Brown Rice)

1. _____
2. _____
3. _____
4. _____
5. _____
6. _____
7. _____
8. _____
9. _____
10. _____
11. _____
12. _____
13. _____
14. _____
15. _____
16. _____
17. _____
18. _____
19. _____
20. _____
21. _____
22. _____
23. _____
24. _____

Joy Eating

Joy Eating is just that—pure and simple joy. This is food you eat because it tastes so good. It doesn't have to do anything helpful in your body and usually it won't, but it tastes good in your mouth. Joy eating includes cake, candy, Doritos, clam dip, popcorn, fettuccine Alfredo, chocolate-chip cookies, and anything else that just tastes wonderful but doesn't do anything for your body. These are foods designed for pleasure, not for nourishment. They are one of the joys in life and your body can handle them in small doses just fine.

I say we need to be able to joy eat. Many diets fail because they don't allow us to live in the real world and enjoy some junk food once in a while. Forget that. I want to go to a birthday party and eat cake; I want to eat candy at Halloween and mashed potatoes with tons of butter on Thanksgiving. There is no way I am willing to completely give these up just to be thin. Naturally thin people do eat for joy some of the time and there is no reason we can't do so as well.

The interesting thing about joy eating is how much joy it can bring us. I have worked with many clients who spend a lot of their time joy eating. They eat because it makes them happy, not because it provides their body with fuel. They go to big, fancy dinners, eat expensive meals, and drink expensive wines. I personally have nothing against this if it is done 10 percent of the time. Whenever I have a client who is doing it much more than this, I know they are getting *too much of their joy in life from food.* I often ask them, "How much of your total life joy comes from food?" (This includes eating at parties, dining out, eating with the family, ice cream trips, and munching popcorn at the movies.) Many times the answer is over 50 percent.

Ask yourself the same question right now. How much of your total life joy comes from food or eating? If you find that your answer is over 50 percent, you have the answer as to why you eat more than your body requires for fuel. It is no wonder you don't want to cut back on eating. It would mean reducing more than half your total joy from life! Ouch!

I had one client who answered 95 percent! It was no wonder she didn't want to stop at 2! This was a big eureka moment for her. As soon as we added more joy to her life that had nothing to do with eating, she was able to reduce her intake of food by almost half and lost weight so quickly it made both our heads spin!

To summarize this point, of all the food you eat, 10 percent of it should be joy eating. Of all the joy in your life, less than 20 percent should come from food. If you are able to maintain this balance and add a lot more joy to your life and a lot more fuel to your body, overeating can be a distant memory.

The secret to joy eating is you must enjoy it. Don't just eat your 10 percent without guilt because now you can. Sit down and savor it! The only reason you are eating this food is to enjoy it, so pick your 10 percent wisely and make sure it is the best thing you can imagine eating, then eat every single bite with awareness and enjoyment. The minute you stop enjoying it, STOP EATING. If you aren't enjoying it, there is no reason it should be in your mouth!

Many of my clients find that this is an "aha" moment for them. They find that they can get a full sense of joy from a food in just a few bites when they really pay attention. They also sometimes find that they didn't enjoy it as much as they thought they would. As soon as you give yourself permission to eat something and the only requirement is that you enjoy it, you lose all the emotional charge of eating a bad food and sometimes that was the whole reason for eating it.

Here are the rules for joy eating:

- Eat for joy 10 percent of the time. This works out to be about one serving a day.
- When possible, try to plan your joy so you make sure you spend your joy-eating time on something you really want to eat.
- You must enjoy each and every bite and you must stop the minute you stop enjoying it or your 10 percent is up—whichever comes first.
- After a "joy-eat," eat again the very next time you get hungry.

By the way, you do not have to be hungry when you "joy-eat," but I promise you, joy food tastes even better when you are.

The following worksheet is a very powerful way to get connected to your eating and your body. I suggest you pick a joy food and do this exercise at least once a week until you are truly connected to what it means to love the food you are eating.

> *Life is too short to not eat some Doritos™ once in a while.*

The Tedious, Powerful Food Worksheet—Part 1

This worksheet is to be used as often as you can handle it. It is very tedious and time consuming, but the results are amazing. Sit down with this one before you eat and document in detail. Pick a Joy or Fuel Food you really like.

Name of Food: _____

Quantity You Want to Eat: _____

Hunger Sensation Scale: (Stomach Fullness)

|_____|
-10   0   10

Describe the Food in Detail: *Look, smell, texture, color, etc.*

_____

_____

_____

Your Feeling before Eating the Food: _____

_____

_____

_____

_____

_____

The Tedious, Powerful Food Worksheet—Part 2

Describe each bite and stop to write in between bites.

Describe bite 1 in detail:_____

Describe bite 2 in detail:_____

Describe bite 3 in detail:_____

Describe bite 4 in detail:_____

Describe bite 5 in detail:_____

Describe bite 6 in detail:_____

Describe bite 7 in detail:_____

Describe bite 8 in detail:_____

Describe bite 9 in detail:_____

Describe bite 10 in detail:_____

Do all the bites taste the same? Yes or No *(Circle one)*

Does it start to taste less pleasurable or more pleasurable as you

add bites? More or Less *(Circle one)*

What is your feeling after ten bites?_____

_____

_____

How much did you want to eat?_____

How much did you eat before feeling satisfied? _____

When did you stop eating?_____

Hunger Sensation Scale:
(Stomach Fullness)

|————————————————————————————————|

-10   0   10

What is your "after" feeling? _____

The Tedious, Powerful Food Worksheet–Part 3

After you have completed the worksheet five or more times, review the sheets for the following trends:

1. Did you over eat more when you were below −2 on the hunger scale? _____

   _____

   _____

2. Were you able to get more satisfied when you paid more attention to each bite?_____

   _____

   _____

   _____

3. How did your feelings affect the quantity of food you ate?

   _____

   _____

   _____

4. Were your before and after feelings the same or different?

   _____

   _____

5. Did you ever stop at bite one because you realized it was not something you wanted to eat?

   _____

   _____

   _____

Fog Eating

Fog Eating is unconscious eating. It's popcorn at the movies, chips in front of the TV, and food out of the pot while cooking. Fog eating is not enjoyable because you hardly realize you are doing it. It's eating when you aren't hungry or eating at a restaurant beyond fullness because you are distracted. Fog eating is a big bummer because you don't need it for fuel and you aren't really enjoying it. I say NEVER fog eat if you can help it. When you eat...eat.

Unfortunately, many of us spend a lot of time here; we are busy eating on the run frenziedly without ever tasting the food we are eating. We have no idea sometimes that we are even doing it. I had one client who ate an entire jar of peanuts and didn't remember eating even one until her hand hit the bottom of the jar and her TV show ended. This is the ultimate insult to yourself. It is like eating behind your own back while you are asleep. It isn't any fun and it's not helping your body. Compare fog eating to pouring juice into a glass. You aren't paying attention so it just flows out of the glass onto the table, onto the floor, and you just keep pouring. You might stop to take the kids to school, then you come back and start pouring again. It is a complete waste.

Pull yourself out of the fog as soon as you catch yourself doing it. Reconnect to yourself and pay attention. This is your life; you don't want to miss it.

Storm Eating

Storm Eating is eating when you aren't hungry, knowing that you are doing it, and feeling unable to stop even though you want to stop.

Storm eating is like binge eating. I call it storm eating so you can know that all storms do end. They feel out of control, but they do end. Storm eating is usually caused by depriving yourself and passing up too many forbidden foods. When you start fueling your body regularly and allowing some joy eating, usually the storm eating disappears.

> When you are in a Storm Eat
> and you feel as if you
> can't stop eating,
> stop and see
> what happens.

Storm eating may also be brought on by intense emotions that feel out of control. I will give you many tools to help you cope with this type of situation in the following chapters.

One of my most memorable storm eats was in college. I was stressed beyond belief because my backpack had been stolen out of my car the week before finals. All of my notes for the entire semester were in that bag and not one thing of value for the thief. I was beside myself with the lose-lose situation. I went to the school store and bought "bin food" (all you storm eaters know that bin food is food sold by weight out of huge containers). I filled up three bags of snack food and went back to my room and ate. I must have eaten fifty yogurt-covered pretzels that day. I seriously cannot even look at one today because I felt so sick. I remember believing I was unable to stop. I felt so helpless and out of control that I was acting my feelings out with the food. I spent the rest of the day being upset about eating so much and feeling sick that I hardly thought about the backpack. I believe now that that was the whole point.

The important thing to remember in a storm is *not to judge yourself*. Every storm eat is caused by a very good reason. You need to be kind to yourself to find out what is going on. Try to observe yourself curiously and

> *Never beat yourself up for overeating. Ever.*

understand why you are doing what you're doing. The damage that occurs from a storm eat is not the amount of calories you eat. The damage is from disconnecting from your body, filling it up past what it is requesting, then beating yourself up for doing it. If nothing else, you must be kind and gentle to yourself. Again, this is a learning opportunity, not an opportunity to make a scary situation worse.

After a storm eat, wait until you're hungry, then eat your fuel food again. It may take you a while to get hungry again after a storm eat. Be patient and trust that your body will let you know when it's time to eat again.

Exercise:

- Make a list of the foods you normally fog eat. Is there a common time of day or place where you are more likely to fog eat?
- Write a description of the last time you storm ate. Can you remember what triggered it? How did you feel afterward?

Eating Tool #4
Waste Some Food

We have been trained not to waste food in the garbage, but to waste it on our bodies. Either way it is wasted. In one way, we just carry the waste with us. Overeating food because we don't want to waste creates fat. It is as if you are telling your body, sorry you aren't still hungry but I paid a lot of money for this and I don't want to throw it away. Can you imagine saying that to a baby? Can you imagine making a little baby eat the rest of its baby food because you didn't want to waste it? No. You wouldn't force feed a baby food it doesn't want and you shouldn't do it to yourself.

This is a very hot issue for many of my clients, and I am always torturing them by making them throw food away. It's either in the garbage or on your body...you decide. I am usually harsh to prove my point. Many of them have had years of programming that they must clean their plate and show respect for the cook by eating what is served. Respect for the cook? Not at the expense of respect for your own body. Never. How your body feels should always come before how the cook feels. Period.

> *Eating food and*
> *being polite should have nothing*
> *to do with each other.*

I had a client, Betty, who couldn't stand to waste food, so she would just eat it. No matter if she was hungry or not, she would clean her plate. If there was food she purchased that she didn't like, she would eat it rather than waste it. She always ate food on a schedule with the food expiration date. As you can imagine, she was overweight and very disconnected with her body and its desires.

I gave her the assignment of buying some large bags of kettlekorn at the farmer's market. I required that she buy much more than she would be able to eat in the short amount of time before they would expire. She reluctantly agreed.

The following night, before she was to go and buy the kettlekorn, she had fitful sleep and felt lots of anger at me surfacing. We talked more about it and she expressed to me how stupid and wasteful she thought the exercise was. I asked her if it was about the money.

She replied that it wasn't, and she would happily pay me the money for the kettlekorn rather than throw it away.

As a coach, I love resistance and increased emotion—it means we are on to something—so I got quite excited and pressed her to do the required exercise.

Apparently very upset, she asked, "Can't I just pretend to buy it?"

I said, "Sure! And you can pretend to lose weight, too." We were both laughing, but the real issue that surfaced was not very funny.

Betty took time to look inside and see what the real issue was and why she felt so strongly about the exercise. What she discovered was a belief system so deep, she didn't even know she had it. When Betty was a teenager, her grandmother had gotten ill and had decided not to go on living by starving herself to death. In an illogical connection, Betty believed that by wasting food, she was throwing away the very thing that could have saved her grandmother's life!

It was a great discovery. She saw how illogical the belief was and used the tools presented later in this book to change it. She can now simply throw food away instead of putting it away on her body. She knows that, either way, it's wasted because it's not being used as fuel.

What is your reason for not wasting food? Is it because of the people starving in the world? Is it because it costs so much? Is it because you want to be a member of the clean-plate club? Whatever your reason is, it is not a good one. If you are going to eat according to your body's wisdom, in our excess culture you are going to have to waste some food. It is a fact. You will consistently be served more than your body will want. Get used to it and start wasting now.

Of course, I do recommend you try and do everything in your power to be responsible and reasonable in how to prepare and order your meals. I am not saying that wasting food is a good thing that should be sought out. I am saying that it really is part of a thin person's life. Try to take precautions against it, but get used to it just the same.

Exercise:

- The next time you order a meal and eat to +2 on the hunger scale and there is quite a bit of food left, throw the rest away. Have the waiter take it and do not request that it be wrapped up. How does this make you feel? What belief system are you onto here? Whose voice do you hear in your head? Is there guilt? I assure you that there is something if you have been eating food rather than wasting it. Find it and write it down.

- Write down how you feel about throwing away perfectly delicious or expensive food when you are not hungry and it will not keep.

- How do you feel about eating this food knowing that your body doesn't need it and it may end up being stored as fat on your body?

When you eat food your body does not require for fuel —you are wasting it, attaching a doggie bag of fat to your hips.

Eating Tool #5
This Ain't Your Mama's Food Journal

I know what you are thinking. "Give me a break! I don't want to write down what I am eating like I am back on some diet and counting calories." I don't blame you. But here is the truth. Of all my clients who lost weight fast, 100 percent of them wrote down what they ate. It is an amazing tool because it forces you to pay attention and stay connected to what you are eating and what category you are eating in.

If I was able to, I would jump off this page right now and grab your shoulders and look you in the eye. I would say that I know you are thinking about skipping this step. I know that you don't think you need to do this part. YOU ARE WRONG. I wrote down every single thing that went into my mouth until I reached my goal weight. At first, it made me feel like a monitored child, but ultimately it taught me more than I ever knew about myself. I didn't do it to count calories or points; I did it to notice my emotional patterns and relationship to my body. It is one of the most powerful tools I know. It is a communication device between you and your body. SO PLEASE DO IT!

Get a small journal and write down what you eat. Write down where you were on the hunger scale and write down what type of eating it was. This is your looking glass into your life. This can be the most powerful tool you have if you are able to look at it with compassion and fascination. There is no judgment. There is no good or bad. These are just interesting facts that have the ability to teach us something about you and your relationship with food.

Keeping a food journal is a powerful tool to keep you awake and connected when you eat.

Here is a sample of one of my journal entries:

Monday

Egg Beaters
Whole-Wheat Toast
Coffee

Started at +2
Ended at -2

Fuel Meal —felt great!

---

2 pieces hard candy

At 2 on hunger scale
It was not a joy eat because I didn't enjoy it.
It was a fog eat—was disconnected from myself
and ate because it was there.

Chicken Breast Sandwich
-2 to 2

Fuel Meal - awesome

Spaghetti
-2 to 5

I started with a fuel and switched to fog...was so
full before I even realized it.
The kids were acting up at the table and I was
feeling stressed. Could have been cause of my
disconnect.

Exercise:

- Pull out your food journal and start it now by writing down everything you have eaten so far today. Try to see of you can connect to where you were on the hunger scale at the time of eating.

Summary of Eating Tools:

- Your body is in charge, so listen to it.
- Fuel eat when you are hungry (at -2) and stop when you are full (at +2) 90 percent of the time.
- Joy eat 10 percent of the time and truly enjoy each bite.
- Eliminate fog eating. Notice when you do it and why.
- Try to find out why you eat in a compassionate way. It's a great tool to get in touch with your emotions.
- Write down everything that goes into your mouth without judgment. Ask yourself why you are eating it.

Never Exercise for Fast Results

"Exercise, but don't ever exercise for the result of losing weight fast. It takes too long and you will quit too soon."

Exercise Tool #1
Never Exercise for Fast Results

*I*n the previous chapter, we talked about how being disconnected from our bodies causes us to overeat. This estrangement from our physical being is what makes it possible for us to gain large amounts of weight without noticing, until we can't fit into our clothes. The first step to reconnect by eating when you are hungry and stopping when you are satiated is the beginning of a new relationship based on cooperation, connection, and love. The second step is exercise.

Many of you aren't even reading this chapter. You are so sick of trying to exercise and dislike it so much you can't imagine that I have anything to say that might make a difference. What I am suggesting is that you change your entire paradigm about exercise as a tool. In my practice, I use exercise as a way to connect to your body, define your priorities, use the emotional strength to stick to them, and to make a significant identity change for the better. My approach to exercise is probably not like any approach you have taken before because I suggest that you don't use it as a tool to lose weight or see immediate results.

I am asking you to make a huge shift from a taker to a giver. If you think about your past attempts at exercise programs or even your current one, I will guess that you are exercising based on what it will give you. Many people "take" from exercise what they can get and this usually leads to not liking it and doing activities that are not enjoyable. I want you to use exercise as a way to give to yourself. The distinction is crucial, and it is not merely semantics. Although, technically, you are the giver and the receiver when you commit to an exercise regime, I want you to start *identifying* only with the giver part of you. You will start giving yourself exercise without expecting anything in return. It may be easy to think of this again as your relationship with your body. You are giving to your body the gift of movement, health, strength, and time. You are letting your body know that it is worth your energy.

I realize that results will come as a by-product of exercise. You will get all the benefits listed later in this chapter that will help you maintain your weight and make you feel better once you get good at it. But these are merely by-products and not the reason you start exercising in the first place. It should feel as if you are making a contribution to your life. You are filling your body with emotional deposits of love. As the giver, it will make you feel good to give. It shouldn't feel like an exhausting drain that doesn't produce any results.

It is something that you are adding to your life, not a burden that is taking away.

People who exercise regularly are communicating to themselves and the world how they should be treated. They are making a statement that they are willing to give to themselves for the sake of giving health and care without so much regard of what they will "get out of it" in terms of losing weight or looking good. Give yourself emotional strength, the ability to overcome excuses, motivation, pride, and the emotional commitment to state that **you matter.**

This approach made the difference when I was trying to lose seventy pounds of fat from my body. It seemed like a huge mountain to climb and I wanted to "take" the results as quickly as I could. I was actually quite greedy in my wanting it right now! I began a pretty serious exercise program, and I worked out like crazy for six weeks and didn't lose one pound! I literally needed help sitting down because I was so sore, but my fat level had not budged. Many people quit at this stage. I remember feeling betrayed by working so hard and not having one thing to show for it. That darn scale had not budged! Instead of giving up, I connected to myself and felt the truth. I knew that I was giving myself an amazing gift by working out everyday. I knew it felt good to be a person who exercised. I knew that I was connecting with the core of my body and loving it by being willing to listen to it and move it. At that moment, I made the decision that I would continue to forge that connection and trust that the results would come. More importantly, if the results didn't come, I knew that I would continue to give to myself in this way. It resonated deep within me that what I was doing made sense because it was coming from within.

What you give, you will receive. Over the next six months, I lost all seventy of those pounds. I developed a relationship with my body that is tight and intimate. This is how I know that I will never gain that weight back. I am not fighting against my body anymore. We listen and live in cooperation with each other. I didn't sell it out for a quick result and I am so proud of that decision. The bonus is that I lost the weight permanently.

When we focus on exercising to lose weight and what it's going to give us, we usually pick exercise that is calorie-burning and usually very hard with little regard to what we might enjoy. We are focused on target heart rates and machine calculations. It's dull and very difficult to do when we are overweight. Then, when the scale doesn't budge, we get frustrated. The personal trainers of the world will disagree with me here, but when you are getting started as a regular exerciser you have to use the psychological approach of contribution not one of "feel the burn."

So, forget exercising to lose weight. I mean it. Don't go for the fat loss results...ever. You will be disappointed. But you must add some kind of exercise to your life that you love. Forget about anything except what really makes you feel good. Make it convenient and something you will be able to maintain for the rest of your life. If you love classes at the gym, then go. If you like walking, then head out your front door and hit the sidewalk or walking path. Try to find something that will beckon to you once you make it a habit. Try out lots of different exercises and see which one you LIKE and not the one you believe will bring you results. The best result you will ever get from exercising is the development of a habit you can use as an emotional tool to relieve stress and connect with your body. That is the ultimate result.

As you begin to exercise, really pay attention to your body and how it feels. It may feel terrible at first. This is not a reason to stop giving to it. The reason it feels hard or tiring is because it has been neglected for so long. Note your feelings, then gently encourage yourself to keep moving. Think about the emotional obstacles you are overcoming. Listen to your body tell you how neglected it feels, how out of shape it is, and how upset it is that you have been ignoring it. Let your body vent. Keep giving. This venting might go on for a few months. You just listen and keep giving. Your body has a right to be upset and, eventually, it will start to trust you and the care you are giving it. Eventually, it will really start to feel good during and after your workout. That is when you know you and your body are finally on the same side. You may not have gotten fast results, you may have had to put up with your body screaming at you, but you have overcome it and that feels amazing! You are an athlete and a regular exerciser and your body thanks you for it.

Exercise:

- How would it feel to be a person who exercises regularly?
- What will it cost you if you don't give yourself this gift?
- How will you stay in the mode of giving to yourself without expectation of results?
- Are you willing to exercise for yourself even if you don't get weight loss results?

Exercise Tool#2
Increase Your Minimum Baseline

Each person has a minimum baseline for how much they work out. For some, it is six days a week for an hour without fail; for others, it's walking from the bed to the refrigerator. What is your baseline level of exercise? This is not what you want or try to do, but instead is what you are committed to doing on a regular basis. It is your standard for fitness. It was what you simply will not tolerate your life without.

Many of us are all or nothing, so we either work out like crazy or not. We either have a gym membership that we use regularly or we don't use it at all. We are either on a regime or we are "currently not making time for it." My suggestion is that you remove this all-or-nothing attitude from your life. I suggest that you never make it possible for you to be sedentary again. You must remove this as an option. Once you start climbing the mountain, you have to promise yourself that you won't ever run back down and sit at the bottom again. You can adjust your intensity, you can climb faster sometimes, and you can slow down at others—but never again let yourself be defined as someone who doesn't work out. I mean it. From this day forward, you must commit to doing something physical at least three times a week.

If you don't have a baseline because you don't work out at all, it's time to make one. This isn't so you will lose weight or benefit health-wise. This is a psychological tool to convince yourself that you are now a person who works out. If you are currently not moving your body at all in a way that resembles exercise, my recommendation is that you exercise a minimum of at least three times a week for five minutes. I know you may think this is too short a time to get any results, but remember, we are not doing it for weight-loss results. We are using this as a way to change your identity, and it really does work. So, the minimum is five minutes and you can build from there. Never again are you allowed to go below the five minutes three times a week. It is a conscious commitment you make to yourself. It may sound easy on paper, but it is even easier to justify and make excuses as to why it can't happen. You may think that, because if it won't make a difference immediately in your physical body, it is not worth doing, but I can assure you that you are wrong. This can be one of the best ways to start connecting to yourself and building your self-esteem.

Make sure you commit to this minimum baseline by writing and putting it on your calendar as an appointment. You are busy during this time and unavailable for anyone else. This is not an appointment that can be rescheduled. This is your appointment with the CEO of your life—you. Just the fact that you make this an important appointment that you have committed to, can change how you feel about yourself. You tell anyone who asks for you at that time, "Sorry, but no." You do not need to provide an explanation that you are going to be exercising. It is an important meeting and if someone asks you to reschedule it, you must reply, "Absolutely not." This resolve will be very powerful in building your motivation and momentum for your commitment to your minimum baseline.

Once you make this commitment, it is much easier to build from here. You start thinking of yourself as someone who works out. If someone asks if you exercise, you can say, "Yes." You can start taking each five-minute segment as a deposit into your self-esteem account. Your body will start to appreciate you more. You will learn the skill of overcoming excuses and obstacles. You will make yourself a priority. You will draw a line in the sand of what you are willing to tolerate. All this for a five-minute commitment! Now you have no reason not to get this done.

Five minutes is all I am asking. You either step outside and start walking or go to the gym and start doing what it is you have decided to do on a regular basis. You must do it for at least five minutes and for three times a week. This does not mean you do it one time a week for fifteen minutes. This does not mean you have to work out hard, sweat, or "feel the burn." This means you do something that looks like your habit of exercise for at least five minutes.

It may be that you get dressed, walk around the block for five minutes and then you stop. That may be all you can muster on some days and that's okay. Other times, you may think it feels nice and you continue to walk or work out for up to an hour and that is great, too. Try not to judge yourself. If you do your minimum...you rock! And you should tell yourself so.

You can pick your minimum time based on what feels do-able for you. It should be a minimum that you can maintain for the rest of your life. There is no reason to judge it—don't say that five minutes won't do enough to make a difference so why bother? This is not about physical results. Do not underestimate the power of the psychological tool; if you do this, it can change the entire way you view yourself. If you cannot find five minutes, three times a week, you have much bigger

> *No one has time
> to work out.
> We have to
> make the time.*

problems than losing weight. Making time for your health and your psychological well-being must be a priority in your life. You are sending a message to yourself that you matter and that you have worth. There is no better way to lose weight than to know you deserve it.

Some of you might feel like you want to set a minimum that is slightly longer, especially if you have been a regular exerciser for a while. The key is making sure it is something you will never fail at. For me, personally, I have a minimum baseline of two days of weight training and two days of a thirty-minute walk per week. This is truly a minimum and quite easy for me to accomplish at this point. I never go below this no matter what is going on in my life. Most of the time, I lift heavy weights four times a week and do an intense cardio six times a week. When I really feel like getting fit for an event or the summer, I will hire a trainer and work out as hard as I can for six to eight weeks. It doesn't work for me to stay at this level continuously, but I do love kicking it hard once in a while. The most important thing is that no matter how hard I have worked over a period of time, I never fall below my minimum baseline. I increase intensity, not time. In fact, the more intense I work out, the less time in the gym it takes.

Having a minimum baseline can change your identity about yourself as a person who exercises. If you stay committed, it can build your self-esteem, your motivation, and your sense of control in your life. So, set it now. Eventually, this will lead you to want to increase the amount of time you spend exercising, but you must start with the minimum.

Exercise:

- What are you committed to setting your minimum baseline to? If this feels intimidating, start at five minutes, three times a week; work up from there. Make sure you write it down and put it as an appointment on your calendar.

Exercise Tool #3
Get Your Shoes On

Once you have established your minimum baseline, you need to commit to it no matter what. There will be many times when you will want to justify missing your appointment. This is NEVER acceptable, no matter what. My clients often tell me that they don't know if they can make this kind of commitment; they don't know if it is possible. When I ask them if they would be willing to make the commitment for $500,000, they admit that they would make it happen for that kind of money. Exactly. *It is possible.* (By the way, I also ask them if they would sell their health for the same amount and all of them have said no way!) So, commit to doing this for something worth more than half a million dollars—your physical and emotional health.

When your feel yourself having good reasons for missing your baseline appointments, make sure you call these reasons what they really are: excuses. There will always be a reason why you can't do it. There will be things that come up that capture your attention that seem more important than a five-minute walk. You will be tired, sick, stressed, and busy. Don't ever let those things come before you and your well-being.

Even if you are faced with responsibilities, even if you have had a terrible day at work, even if you haven't slept very well...GET YOUR SHOES ON! Put your shoes on and go outside and walk no matter what. It seems that if you can take the first step, no matter how hard it is, and put your shoes on, you can do your workout even if it's just for five minutes. It can be the one constant in your life. It can be the thing you do for YOU no matter what else happens.

Excuses belong on paper and not in your life. If you have an excuse, write it down. I give my clients lists numbered 1–50 and I ask them to fill it up during our time together. I tell them that they can have excuses, but they need to write them down and then get their shoes on. Fill up the page with excuses, then fill up your life with fulfilled commitments to yourself.

Here are some samples of excuses that look really good on paper:

I don't have time.	*I am too busy.*
I didn't sleep well.	*I have to clean.*
I have to take care of my kids.	*I am exhausted.*
I have to work.	*I just want to relax.*
I deserve a break.	*I am in pain.*
I am sick, and I don't feel good.	*I am lazy.*

It's all or nothing.　　　　*I already blew it.*
I am not good at it.　　　*It's boring.*
I don't feel like it.

My favorite client excuse, and by far the most common one I hear, is that there isn't enough time. Twenty-four hours is enough. We all have twenty-four hours no matter how busy or important we are. The truth is we all have enough time, we just chose not to use it. My trainer opens his gym at 3:30 a.m. and the place is packed. These people are making time. They are not accepting excuses. They are not being victims of their schedule, but rather taking control and making the time they need. The truth is that most of us don't need to work out in the middle of the night to accomplish our minimum. It is time to check your priorities. Psst. Without your health, you are not here, and then you really don't have any time.

This process will allow you to flex some physical muscle on a regular basis, but it will also provide you with an amazing emotional and motivational tool to take control of your own life and never hand your power over to an excuse again.

Excuse Strategies

Pick your top-5 legitimate good excuses that you feel are justified.

Sample Excuse:
I am way too busy to exercise tomorrow.. I have to work and then pick up the kids and then go to a Christmas party for my husband's work. I will barely have time to breathe-let alone exercise.

How can I use this excuse to my advantage and turn it into a strategy or strength?
I can use this as an oppportunity to prove to myself that no matter how much I do for others or how busy the day is, I can find time for myself. I will wake up an hour earlier and go for a walk before I begin my day. This will make me feel proud of myself and less resentful that I don't have time for myself.

Excuse #1 _____
How can I use this excuse to my advantage and turn it into a strategy or strength?

_____

_____

_____

_____

Excuse #2: _____
How can I use this excuse to my advantage and turn it into a strategy or strength?

_____

_____

_____

Excuse #3: _____
How can I use this excuse to my advantage and turn it into a strategy or strength? _____

_____

_____

_____

Excuse #4: _____
How can I use this excuse to my advantage and turn it into a strategy or strength? _____

_____

_____

_____

Excuse #5: _____
How can I use this excuse to my advantage and turn it into a strategy or strength? _____

_____

_____

_____

*Excuses are
dream stealers
and health killers.*

Exercise Tool #4
Know the Health Benefits/Risks

For some reason, we are not motivated to exercise for our health. We have all heard the statistics about disease and obesity and exercise and prevention. Yet, this doesn't seem to motivate us to work out. Again, when I ask my clients if they would exercise daily for 500k, they say of course they would. When I ask them if they would trade their health for the same amount, they say no way! Yet, they won't exercise for health. It is baffling. It is evidence of how low many of us put our own well-being on the our to-do list. The most effective thing we can do to prevent disease is to exercise and eat fuel. But exercise is usually the first thing to be eliminated from a busy day, over soccer practice, the dentist, and birthday parties!

I am going to list many of the health benefits to exercising and the health risks if you don't exercise. You still may be motivated only by the size of your jeans, but I think it is worth mentioning what it can do for your physical and emotional life. It can be the physical manifestation of how you feel about yourself and your time on this planet. Without your health, you have nothing. You may not even be here, so please read these benefits and risks and really let them sink in. Don't go into emotional denial and think that none of these problems can happen to you. Most women die from a heart disease, and their first heart attack is usually their last. By doing what you can to prevent this tragedy, you are showing yourself that you matter.

On the facing page is a list of the **benefits of aerobic exercise**. This includes walking, running, treadmill, or any other activity that increases your heart rate.

Read each one carefully.

Exercise:

Using the following list, make a list of all the current benefits you are experiencing due to the amount of time you spend exercising. If you don't exercise, make a list of the health issues you currently have or are at risk for.

Two-thirds of women who have a heart attack have no warning. This can be your warning.

Benefits of Aerobic Exercise.

Increases stamina
Flush toxins
Improves quality of sleep
Makes the heart stronger
Reduces body fat
Facilitates physical activity
Reduced risk of depression
Increase HDL
Lowers risk of
  • High blood pressure
  • Stroke
  • Diabetes
  • Colon cancer
  • Breast cancer
  • Arthritis
  • Sleep apnea
Improves your focus
Heightens your productivity
Improves your energy
Releases anxiety
Helps maintain weight loss
Lung fitness
Connects you to your body and helps you listen to it
Gives sense of general well-being

Not only is it very important to start doing something aerobically for the listed reasons, it is equally important to lift weights. If you don't want to worry about gaining weight as you get older, you MUST lift weights. I am not talking about two-pound dumbbells here; I am talking about some serious weights that can change your strength and your body. As you get older, you lose muscle, which means you can gain weight faster than you do now. Furthermore, lifting weights is the only way you can truly change your body shape. It isn't just taking your current body and making it smaller. Over the long term, lifting weights for a while can cause you to catch a glimpse of yourself in the mirror and see that your body has changed literally before your eyes.

Lifting weights is also a great way to see progress and increase your emotional and physical strength. When I first started lifting, I was weak and sore most of the time. But as I kept lifting heavier weights I felt stronger and stronger and literally saw my muscles grow. No, I did not bulk up and start looking like a man. Big muscles make your body smaller not bigger. Fat makes your body bigger because it takes up room; muscles take up less room and make your body look lean and firm, so please don't be afraid to lift heavy weights. Get someone to show you how to lift properly, and then lift as heavy as you can. The point is to break down the muscle each time you lift so it will rebuild bigger and stronger than it was before. You cannot do this when you are lifting one-pound weights with very little effort. As your muscles increase in size, they require more calories than fat just to rest, so it helps you burn even more fat.

Benefits of Weight Lifting

Prevents injuries
Reduces LDL
Reduces risk of
• Diabetes
• Cardio disease
• Osteoporosis
• Some cancers
Reverse aging process by counteracting
• Decreased mobility
• Loss of balance
• Joint instability
• Loss of muscle tissue
Helps you stay leaner
Body uses more calories through the day to sustain muscle
Raises BMR-every pound of muscle burns approx an additional 50 calories per day
Feeling strong is empowering
You can eat more
You look toned
You can change the entire shape of your body
It increases mental focus

I know I am not a personal trainer and this book is mainly on the emotional part of losing weight, but I would feel as if I was leaving out a secret if I didn't tell you that you MUST LIFT WEIGHTS. The results are slow and sometimes a little painful, but the strength you gain emotionally and physically is more than worth it.

If there were a pill that could promise all these things, it would be worth millions of dollars. Yet, we can have it for FREE! We can have all these benefits for no money, just a little time and personal effort.

Exercise:

- Go to a gym or buy a book and learn about the main muscle groups and the exercises that you can do to strengthen them. Practice the form until you have it perfectly. Then, complete each of the exercises at the heaviest weight you can tolerate for ten reps. Write down what that weight is in your journal. Set a one-month goal for increasing that weight by a few pounds, then see how much progress you can make.

Exercise Tool #5
Bribery

Another psychological technique that I think is price-less is self-bribery. I highly recommend it as long as it doesn't involve food. The truth of the matter is that some days exercise just isn't something you are look-ing forward to. You can understand all the health benefits, have a plan, and ignore all your excuses; but sometimes you just need a little extra incentive to get yourself going. Bribing yourself with a reward or avoidance of a consequence can be very effective.

Here are some of my ideas:

- I love "People Magazine," but I only read it when I am on the bike at the gym.
- I also read books I love when biking on the stationary bike.
- I put awesome music on my i-pod and listen to it.
- I pick a nice outdoor area to walk in and breathe and enjoy the scenery.
- I listen to books on tape as I am walking.
- I buy cute workout outfits and only let myself wear them when I am working out.
- I exercise with a friend so we can catch up.
- I hire a personal trainer.

- I pick an aerobics class that has high energy.
- I join a gym that has great activities for my kids so they can have a break from me.
- I tell my dog I am taking him on a "hike," and he gets so excited. I won't let him down.
- I have put a chart on the wall with my exercise appointments and I cross them off when completed. After a certain number of workouts, I go in for a spa treatment.

Ask yourself what you can do to make your exercise more enjoyable. Rate your exercise event on a scale from one to ten. One means you are dreading it and ten means you can't wait to get it going. Once you have your number, turn on your creative genius and ask yourself what you could do to make it three points higher? For example, if you are planning to take a walk and you have many excuses and you're at about a 2 in terms of looking forward to it, ask yourself what you could do to make it a 5. Maybe you could load a great motivating book on CD into your CD player and that increases your excitement about it. Maybe you could call your neighbor and ask if she wants to come with you. Maybe you could have the kids get on their bikes and ride next to you. Maybe you could pick a spot that is prettier than your current plan. Once you get to 5, you will be more motivated to make it happen. You know that you have already committed to it; you might as well make it as enjoyable as possible.

Many of my clients use negative consequences as a last-ditch effort to commit to the schedule of working out. They send me an email every time they work out and every time they hit their workout baseline. They develop a sense of accountability by giving me their word that they will make it happen. They want to avoid the feeling of not keeping a promise, so they get it done. I say, do whatever works for you. Never underestimate the power of getting someone to partner with you. Trainers and coaches can be an awesome tool. They can help you set high standards, break through excuses, and make you commit to a time and place. I have had various trainers and each time I hire one, they push me beyond what I am capable of in my own mind (I actually pay him to specifically do this for me!). Then, I do what he says without question because I don't want to waste my investment. Every little bit of bribery helps.

Exercise:

- Make a list of five bribes you could use on yourself to help you exercise.

Exercise Tool #6
Be Willing to Suck at It

Anything physical you do when you are overweight is going to be difficult. All my clients who have as much weight to lose as I did, hate moving their fat bodies. I get it. It sucks to have fat rolls get in the way of a leg press. It's awful trying to catch your breath after moving up a hill because your body weight is so heavy. Know that it will suck. Know that once you start losing weight, it will suck less. Once you make a commitment to doing a little exercise consistently, it will get easier and easier UNLESS YOU STOP COMPLETELY. Don't ever stop doing your baseline. Keep going. Keep going. Suck at it. Suck at it. Suck at it. Think about what it feels like to suck at it. On the other side of sucking at it, however, is being good at it. You have to go all the way though the process, so don't be surprised when it's difficult.

So many of my clients come to me and say they don't want to set foot in a gym or try a new class. They tell me they are intimidated by the machines and the pace of the classes. I always tell them, "Of course you are! Now, go sign up!" Life is not about being good at everything and only doing things we already know how to do. Life can be about growth and learning and getting better each day. It makes us feel young and alive when we are willing to take risks and be a beginner. It makes us feel silly not to know how to use a machine when it seems every little toned body in the gym knows how to use it perfectly. This is not an excuse not to try. I love watching my kids try new things. They just go for it. They could care less how silly they look. They want to learn and grow and try and get better. You can be just like this if you are willing to start where you are and encourage yourself each time. It builds courage, it helps you overcome fear, and it develops your individual source of control because you don't pay attention to what anyone else thinks. You aren't in the gym to prove anything to anyone but yourself.

A good example of me being willing to suck really bad is when I learned how to play golf. I wanted to learn how to golf so I could hang out with my husband. He

> *Being willing to suck at things is one secret to an excitement-filled life.*

loves to go golfing, but it's a sport that takes half the day and he was always gone for a long time. I decided that I would learn the sport in order to spend more time with him. Any of you who play know that it truly is the most frustrating sport ever created. It took me three years of sucking at it before I would keep score. It was awful to tee off in front of people and have the ball go three feet. Fortunately, I wasn't golfing to impress anyone; I wasn't golfing so I could look good and not make mistakes. I was learning to golf so I could try a new sport and to spend more time with my husband, so I didn't let anything like being horrible at it make me quit. I am still pretty bad, but I can go and be with my husband and actually play. I decided I would rather be a beginner in the game than a spectator on the sidelines; it has paid off in so many ways that I apply to the rest of my life. It's a very good skill set to have. I now try lots of new things because I know how to suck at things in the beginning and it doesn't bother me.

The following advice, from my own brilliant teacher, Martha Beck, sums it up, "Anything worth doing is worth doing terribly." Now go.

Exercise:

- Think of something you really want to do but have avoided because you don't think you will be any good at it. Maybe it's trying a yoga or pilates class, maybe its learning to lift weights or get a black belt in karate; whatever it is, write it down. Write down what it would mean to try this out and be a beginner and do it just terribly. Write down what you are afraid of. Write down the worst-case scenario. Now, get your shoes on and go do it.

You will never learn to be an expert at anything if you aren't willing to suck at it first.

Feelings Are for Feeling

"There isn't a feeling out there that can kill you if you are willing to actually feel it."

Feeling Tool #1
Be Willing to Feel and Not Run from Your Feelings

As children, we sometimes experience things that cause intolerable emotions. We learn at a very young age how to cope by not feeling. Many of us distract ourselves by eating. Some of us obsess about our weight instead of feeling terrified of our life. As adults, we are now able to feel our emotions. We have the emotional maturity to feel and know that we have some control over the feelings and we understand the cause of them. As adults, we know that feelings do end and that they don't have the power to kill us.

Or do we?

Many of us haven't made this step into adulthood. We spend our lives stressing, eating, and obsessing about our bodies instead of just feeling our feelings. We run and run and run because we think we might not survive them. The truth is that we won't survive them if we keep on running away from them. We need to learn how to feel.

Emotional adulthood requires that we live in the now and face our present emotional condition whatever it happens to be. Feeling stress and anxiety on a regular basis lets you know that you are running away from yourself and your emotional life. It is time to jump in.

Many books and approaches recommend removing the triggers that cause you to feel the stress. I say seek them out. Any time your emotion increases from a trigger is a wonderful opportunity for you to feel what comes up for you. Pay attention. Get to know your feelings. Learn from each feeling. Each feeling will take you deeper into the knowledge of yourself if you follow it in. When you deny feeling an emotion, you deny yourself the opportunity to learn *why you are feeling the feeling* in the first place and with that you miss the opportunity to change the cause of it. Don't be afraid of knowing who you really are. You, with all your feelings, are amazingly marvelous.

> *Many of us spend a good part of our day avoiding and ducking negative emotions.*
> *What a waste of energy!*

Any feeling that comes into our day or our life needs to be welcomed. We need to look forward to our feelings and learn how to "do" them well. I am always telling this to my clients. We can "do" embarrassment. We can "do" shame. We can "do" pain. What I mean by this is that there is nothing to be afraid of. Instead of running, we can let the feelings come in and get to know them. We get to know what pain feels like in our body. We get to know how it feels in our mind. We go through the feeling to the other side of it, and then it's gone. You don't have to eat when you feel. You don't have to fight stress and anxiety and worry about feeling emotions. We don't have to avoid situations that make us feel, because we aren't afraid of them anymore.

It sounds simple, but the skill of being able to feel all your feelings can completely change your life. Your knowledge of how to feel and your willingness to feel will increase your likelihood of taking risks and living more fully. Having courage doesn't mean you aren't afraid, it means you feel afraid and you do it anyway. You and fear can become friends once you get to know each other. Many of the things I do in my life and my business scare me, but I don't get scared of being scared. I just say "Hello scared, I was expecting you to come; now let's get to work."

> *When you fight against feeling a negative emotion —*
> *you actually make it stronger.*

Sitting at a kitchen table and feeling a feeling all the way through, instead of eating, is a very courageous act. When the fear starts to come and we recognize it as fear, we need to sit and watch it come. Welcome it. Expect it. Don't run to the refrigerator and start eating so you can forget about it. Don't start thinking about how fat you are. Stay with this feeling right now and acknowledge it. It really can't hurt you if you let it in to wash over you. If you start to resist it or fight with it or try to deny it, it will cause you additional pain in your life. I like to use the example of someone coming to your house to break in. If you aren't expecting them and they sneak in the back door and you pretend they aren't there, they can cause you harm. But, if you are expecting them and you are sitting calmly on the couch with a couple of police officers, it's not so bad. You let the guy come in and you watch him leave peacefully with the police.

Many of my friends and family have told me they believe I am fearless because I am willing to take big risks. The truth is I know that when I set a big, hairy goal, part of the deal is that I am going to feel some fear. I expect it to come and I am not surprised when it arrives. I allow myself to feel the fear and I keep moving forward. It is like I know fear will be my companion and I have learned how to work with it and yield to it instead of deny it or fight it. I like to keep it close, not buried under fat or food. Fear only becomes an issue when we avoid feeling it. We avoid taking a risk because we don't want to feel it; we bury the feeling under stress, anxiety, or fat.

Exercise:

* Make a list of the top three negative feelings you avoid feeling. What do you believe would happen if you let yourself feel them?

> *What is the worst thing that could happen if you allow yourself to feel a feeling?*

Feeling Tool #2
What Are You Feeling Right Now?

Each time you have an urge to eat when you are not hungry or overeat past fullness, stop for one full minute and ask yourself what you are feeling. "I don't know" is not an acceptable answer. Go in and find it. There is an emotion that is signaling you to eat when you aren't hungry and the first step is to find out what it is. One of my clients asked me, "What do you expect me to do when all the anxiety and fear comes up?" Feel it. Find the feeling and feel it. Go into it.

As you are going through your day, ask yourself what are you feeling now? How are you feeling at this very moment? If you think it's stress or anxiety, sit with the idea that it's a cover emotion. What is underneath the anxiety? What is underneath the stress? If you feel like you want to eat, ask yourself why? If you feel like you're unhappy because you are fat, guess again. There is a real feeling that is inside you. Find out what it is.

Whenever I have a client who is filled with anxiety and stress, I know I have a "runner"—someone who is distracting him/herself from the reality of life by living on stress. Stress is a way of not feeling. We may feel afraid of feeling hurt so we feel fear of feeling the emotion instead. That just makes us anxious about feeling the fear of feeling the feeling. It's exhausting. While it's easy for me to say, "Just feel the real feeling and be done with it," this isn't an easy task for many people to accomplish. I have clients who tell me they have to eat in order to calm down. What they are really doing is trying to distract themselves from the anxiety. Just feel the REAL feeling and be done with it. The food struggle and the anxiety about our weight is a decoy. Stressing out about every little thing is a distraction from the real stuff in our real lives. When we connect to our real feelings, we connect to our true selves. When we are connected to our true selves, we get to be connected to our true sources of pain and joy. Anxiety is a choice and not a good one.

On the following page is a list of emotions you might feel. Discover which ones you have right now or during the day. Ask yourself regularly, "What is going on?" Stay connected. I am asking you to really think—what are your feelings at this very moment? Again, "I don't know" is not an acceptable answer. Look within yourself. Dig deep. Find it. What is going on?

Feelings List

Intensity of Feelings	HAPPY	SAD	ANGRY	CONFUSED
HIGH	Elated Excited Overjoyed Thrilled Exuberant Ecstatic Fired Up Delighted	Depressed Disappointed Alone Hurt Left Out Dejected Hopeless Sorrowful Crushed	Furious Enraged Outraged Aggravated Irate Seething	Bewildered Trapped Troubled Desperate Lost
MEDIUM	Cheerful Up Good Relieved Satisfied Content	Heartbroken Down Upset Distressed Regret	Upset Mad Annoyed Frustrated Agitated Hot Disgusted	Disorganized Foggy Misplaced Disoriented Mixed Up
MILD	Glad Content Satisfied Pleasant Fine Mellow Pleased	Unhappy Moody Blue Sorry Lost Bad Dissatisfied	Perturbed Uptight Dismayed Put Out Irritated Touchy	Unsure Puzzled Bothered Uncomfort- able Undecided Baffled Perplexed

The worst feeling in the world
is still just a feeling –
nothing more.

The other main distinction to consider when you are determining what you are feeling is the difference between a sensation and a feeling. In the first chapter, I had you get in touch with your sensations of hunger in your body when it requires fuel. There will also be times when your body has the emotion of hunger when you are hungry for something besides food. This is a very important distinction that can help immensely when trying to stop eating for emotional reasons. If, at any time, you feel hungry and you are above 0 on the hunger scale, you are probably hungry for something besides food. Go in and find it. See if you can find a way to satisfy it with something besides food. If you are unable to satisfy the hunger, be willing to allow it. Hunger does not need to be a scary emotion. It is very natural for us to be hungry for things we want and believe we need in our life. We don't need to eat over it or run from it. We can do "hungry." We can sit with our emotional hunger and come to the realization that if we are hungry for companionship, no amount of cheesecake will do the trick. Cheesecake, or any other food for that matter, cannot substitute for the love of another human being or our own self-love. Don't be afraid of your hungers. See them.

The Now Feeling Worksheet

What am I feeling? (e.g., worried-no one will ever read this book)

_____

_____

_____

_____

Where is it in my body? (e.g., my neck, back, my stomach)

_____

_____

_____

_____

Is there another feeling underneath this one? (e.g., fear)

_____

_____

_____

_____

What does it make me want to do? (e.g., hide and not publish this book))_____

_____

_____

_____

_____

What memories does this feeling trigger? (e.g., when I was a young girl trying to gain acceptance) _____

_____

_____

_____

_____

What is my opinion of this feeling? (e.g., I think it is unfounded and based on my own unproven speculation about what might happen and not based on fact) _____

_____

_____

_____

Why am I feeling it? (e.g., I have an illogical thought that if no one reads this book it will mean I am less worthy as a person or a coach)

_____

_____

_____

_____

Am I trying to fight or bury this feeling? (e.g., yes-by complaining to my husband about how hard it is to write and how much I hate it, when I am really just experiencing fear) _____

_____

_____

_____

_____

Could I just allow it to be here without reacting? (e.g., Yes. When I let the fear just wash over me I can admit to myself and my husband that I am afraid. I don't have to talk myself out of it. I can just sit with fear and as I do it slowly fades.) _____

_____

_____

_____

_____

Feeling Tool #3
Reacting vs. Feeling Your Feelings

When I start telling clients to feel their feelings, they inevitably start telling me how this is impossible. They can't imagine a life where they are feeling their feelings all the time. They imagine that they will be walking around, crying and screaming and yelling. They say things like, "So, when I am in the middle of a very big meeting, you want me to just feel?" Yes. Yes and Yes. I want you to stay connected to yourself at all times and acknowledge your feelings.

What is the alternative? Not feeling? Being riddled with stress? You must feel what you are feeling *in the moment.* You must stay connected to yourself and your body. The point at which you disconnect is when you overeat. The difference here is that I am not suggesting that you *react* to your feelings in a physical way. Many times we feel a feeling and believe we must "do" something about that feeling right away by acting it out or expressing it. This simply just isn't true. You can allow yourself to feel angry and you can notice that the anger makes you want to punch your boss, but you can stand quietly and be fascinated by this without ever taking a swing. You may not show your boss anger at all, but that does not mean you don't show the anger to yourself. You can use the anger as a way into yourself. You can look at the anger and wonder why it has come up. You can explore what belief is causing it. You can look at the situation from a very kind perspective with acknowledgement and care and no one needs to know if you don't want them to.

By not reacting to the anger, you can use your creative mind to come up with a way to act that would be appropriate and useful for you. You can stay calm while you are evaluating the anger. Fresh anger will not overwhelm you if you don't fight with it. Buried anger may be a little more challenging because it has been festering in your denial of it. You still allow it to come up and you work through the feelings worksheet and you don't let it run you around. You are the one in charge and, although you are willing to pay attention and listen to what it has to say, you are not going to let it run you or cause you to take action on its behalf without your consent. In very few cases, is there ever an upside to expressing and displaying anger. Usually, when we allow anger to surface without reacting, we realize that what is really going on is fear and we can explore this idea before we decide to act on it. Truly, feelings can come, be acknowledged, and be evaluated without anyone around you even noticing. It is the balance of not stuffing/denying and not reacting or acting it out. It is right in the middle and it is called feeling.

A perfect time to ask yourself what you are feeling is when you get to +2 on the hunger scale and stop eating. Put your fork down for one full minute and check in with your emotions. What are you feeling? Just notice. Be fascinated. Feel the feeling and get to know it. Let it swim around in your body without judging it. This is you, uncensored and paying attention. This is the first step to taking control of your emotional life.

The reason it is imperative for us to stay connected and feel, is so we can be aware of how much our feelings and our avoidance of feeling is running our lives

Imagine a door with the feeling written on it. Instead of trying to hold the door closed – open it and walk into the "room" of your feeling.

and driving our actions. Many of us are living in a dodge-ball game, running through our lives trying to avoid the many negative emotions that are coming at us. By fighting the emotion, we are giving it power over us. We are letting the emotion dictate how we exercise, how we risk, whom we talk to, where we go, and when we stop eating. The anxiety comes, and we fight it by eating. The sadness comes, and we react to it by not working out. The fear comes in, and we decide not to take the risk. All of these emotions become dream stealers, dictating how we will live and how much we will weigh.

Emotional strength, to me, does not mean that you don't feel negative emotions. Emotional strength means that you are in charge of your emotions because you don't pretend they are not there and you don't try to go to war with them. You put down your weapons and you pay attention to them and listen to what they are trying to tell you. It is a peaceful coexistence when you are listening attentively and respecting the emotions, but you ultimately have the final say on the action you take.

Having weak emotional strength is living a life of fighting feelings and running away. It is like telling a lie about what you are really feeling, then having to live with the lie and make up more lies to cover the first one. Moderate emotional strength is feeling emotions sometimes, but only when convenient. True solid, emotional strength is a peaceful, loving connection to yourself and all of your feelings. There is no judgment in what comes up. It is just acknowledged. You are deeply aware of everything you are feeling and you decide whether or not the feeling will be in charge. You use the feelings to go deeper into who you are and why you are feeling this way. Then, you decide exactly how to live and take action despite them or in honor of them.

Exercise:

- Name a time when you allowed yourself to feel a feeling without reacting to it.
- Name a time you tried to avoid feeling and ended up reacting strongly anyway.

You can feel your feelings without acting them out.

Feeling Tool #4
Fat Is Not a Feeling

How many times have you said that you feel fat? As if fat were an emotion or a way of being. You can have fat on your body, but you cannot be fat or feel fat. Your true being is weightless. You cannot just be your body. You cannot be your fat. Fat does not reside as an emotion in your psyche. Fat is merely tissue, stored potential energy.

My clients argue with me on this one, but when you are "feeling fat" you are really feeling something else. Fat is another decoy emotion. It's a good substitute for what is really going on with you. Go deeper. Look inside. Go beyond the fat: it's a cheap substitute. What are you really feeling? Look at the list of emotions on the table and notice that fat is not one of them; decide which one you're really going through.

I will give you an example of how many of us use fat as a substitute for really connecting to ourselves. One of my clients lives alone and is newly divorced. She noticed that when she came home from work, she always went into the kitchen and started eating whether she was hungry or not. She usually ate a large quantity of food, beat herself up for eating it, then groaned about how fat she was. When we looked at this in detail, we noticed that coming home to an empty house brought up a feeling of loneliness. When she saw loneliness coming, she ran to the kitchen and ate. She then fiercely judged and berated herself for eating and reminded herself how fat she was. And it worked! She didn't feel lonely at all! She was able to distract herself into feeling fat so loneliness was the furthest thing from her mind. If she could allow the loneliness to come and really let herself feel it, she would be connecting to what is true for her. She could then explore the cause of the loneliness, the belief system that is presenting it, and understand how she can be lonely without eating. She would discover that feeling lonely is not such a horrible thing that she can't live through. She would understand that she could survive a little loneliness and come out healthy and strong on the other side. She would know that there is life after loneliness. If she allowed lonliness, she wouldn't need to eat to distract herself from it. She could peacefully meet it head on.

Lonliness is just a feeling, not a state of being.

Know that your feelings about your weight and the feeling you create from overeating or depriving yourself are engaging you in a decoy struggle. It is a distraction from your real emotional life. It gets you thinking about food and your weight instead of what is really going on under the surface. Most of us former dieters are afraid of being deprived. We believe that trying to lose weight means that we will be deprived of joy, connection, foods we love, or a sense of belonging. Many diets that restrict us from eating in a normal way exacerbate these feelings. We have to prepare or order tasteless food. We can't join in with cocktails or dessert and we can't relax because we have to stay in control to prevent a slip in our diet. Unfortunately, to many of us, this is a familiar feeling. We may have grown up feeling disconnected from people around us in our families or in our schools. We use diets to repeat this pattern; isolation ensues. We believe deprivation feels awful. Deprivation from food is one thing, but deprivation from love and connection is worse. Most often, we deprive ourselves of our own love, time, and nurturing. Each time we try to feel, we rebel, playing this rebellion out by overeating. It's good for immediate gratification, but bad for our long term happiness. This great drama can fill our minds and keep us distracted quite well.

Your real work on this planet is not your weight or your fat. The fabric of your emotional journey is not about deprivation and overeating. It is about love and fear and manifesting the magnificent person you already are. It is time to pay attention to your real life. Stop distracting yourself from your emotional life. Find out what you are feeling and feel it. It is then that you can find the way to who you really are. I promise you, it is not just fat.

Exercise:

- Remember the last time you felt fat. Can you identify what you were really feeling?

Life is not supposed to be about feeling positive emotions all the time. Negative emotions are part of life – plan on them coming and willingly experience each one.

Feeling Tool #5
All Feelings Come from within Us

If you can understand and apply this section, you can justify the price you paid for this book. Of all the tools I give my clients, this is one with which they always have the most aha moments. You must understand that there seems to be two different reasons we feel. One reason we feel is because we have a deeply rooted belief system that comes from within us; it presents us with a negative feeling when we might have nothing negative happening in our life. Maybe we were having a perfectly good day, but we feel depressed. This is an internal emotion because it came from within and wasn't connected to our outside world. Embrace it, feel it, and find the belief system that caused it.

The other type of feeling we experience is caused by external circumstances—or so we think. We really chose to allow the circumstances to cause us to feel a certain way. We go to work and something stressful happens, then we are suddenly stressed. Someone looks at us funny and we are suddenly embarrassed. Another person might be angry with us and we feel angry at them too. We believe that the circumstance caused the feeling. What really happened is that we decided to feel a certain way because of the circumstances.

The truth is you decide how you are going to feel based on what you believe about yourself and what you believe about the circumstances of your life. Many times, we are confused and believe that the real reason we are mad is because of something someone said to us. But the real reason we are mad is because we *believed them.* We have interpreted the event in a way that brought up a negative emotion from within. Here are some samples:

- *Possible Thought*: "My husband makes me so mad."
  Reality: No, you make you mad.

- *Possible Thought*: "My body makes me feel so ugly."
  Reality: No, you make you feel so ugly

- *Possible Thought*: "She really hurt my feelings."
  Reality: No, you chose to feel hurt.

- *Possible Thought*: "My life makes me unhappy."
  Reality: No, you make you unhappy.

- *Possible Thought*: "This illness has ruined my life."
  Reality: No, your reaction ruined your perspective.

Once you get to know that you have control over your own emotional life, you realize that all the emotions you feel and actions you take are your responsibility. When we start to look into what is causing our feelings, we learn that we are causing them by our own belief systems and our own unwillingness to pay attention. If we allow our emotional life to really live in its truth, then we can decide if we want to continue to feel a certain way or not by changing the actual cause of the feeling.

The good news about this is if you are responsible for all your emotions, you can become responsible for the actions that cause them and change. You acknowledge the feeling and feel it without reacting, and then you determine what you are doing to cause it so you can chose to do something differently. For example, if someone says something mean to you, you can chose to not believe it. You can choose to go into yourself and find what you really believe. Many times, I believe that other people's unsolicited opinions of me are none of my business; it is my opinion that matters.

Each thing in life only has the meaning you give it. How you choose to interpret an event can determine how you will feel. In the next chapter, you will learn that how we interpret events is determined by what we believe. Changing disempowering belief systems can cause us to feel much more joy and much less pain in our lives. It truly is completely within our control no matter what the circumstance is we might be facing.

Exercise:

- Is there someone or something you blame regularly for how you feel? What does it feel like to take back the responsibility for how you feel in each and every moment?

No circumstance or person is ever responsible for how you feel.

What you think or believe about the circumstance or person is what causes your feelings.

Feeling Tool #6
Be a Happy Person
Experiencing a Negative Situation.
Don't Become the Negative Situation

Most people wake up in the morning and wonder what kind of day they are going to have. They wonder what might happen to them that will determine how they feel that day. Not me. I wake up and decide today will be a good day no matter what happens out there. I am a happy person and I own the ability to remain that way. I can be happy at my core and go through a negative experience. I can feel a negative emotion all the way through and decide that it will not be the emotion I live by that day. I can be peaceful in the most stressful of circumstances. I am not saying you decide to fake being happy, rather that you actually *decide* to be happy.

I know. You are thinking, "Easier said than done." But really it's not. Many clients tell me they have a very stressful life. I ask them what that has to do with how they feel. Your life may be chaotic, but that doesn't mean you have to be. Other clients have told me they are annoyed by someone they work with. I tell them the same thing. You can be a peaceful woman in a room with an annoying person. You can acknowledge that you feel annoyed, decide not to react to it, and chose to be peaceful.

I am always suggesting to my clients that instead of reacting to people, they become fascinated by them. Isn't it interesting how selfish, annoying, demanding, and mean people can be? It has nothing to do with you and everything to do with them and you can separate from it and be fascinated without taking it on. Don't absorb the feelings of the people around you. Don't become the experience you are having. You decide what's to happen during your day; don't let it decide what's going to happen to you. Furthermore, decide to choose what happens to your life and not let your life happen to you.

Even if you are experiencing divorce, weight gain, obesity, or being fired, you can remain who you are at your essence and see the situation for what it is. You don't need to let your past experiences or current circumstances define you. It is separate from who you are. You truly are a spiritual being having a worldly experience. Remember, you can take all action from a place of peacefulness and reduce the belief systems that cause you to feel negative feelings in the first place.

Exercise:

- Make a list of everyone and everything in your life that you believe is causing you pain. For example, "My husband causes me to feel unloved because he isn't romantic." Make the list with as many things as you can think of.

- Now, go through the list and rewrite the reasons by taking full responsibility for them. For example, "I chose to feel unloved because my husband isn't romantic." Or, "I chose to feel ugly because I weigh three hundred pounds." Or, "I chose to feel weak because I overate yesterday."

- Could you decide to feel differently about people or circumstances? Could you remain happy despite the negative situation? Why or why not?

> *Realizing you are responsible for your own feelings is very good news. It means you don't have to rely on someone else to feel better.*

What You Believe Is Who You Are

"Every single negative feeling is caused by a belief we have. Change the belief and you lose the feeling."

Belief Tool #1
Beliefs Are the Foundation for Our Identity

I have not had an easy life, but I do believe I have had the life I was meant to have. My parents were divorced when I was young; my mother was severely depressed and my dad was busy having an affair. As a teenager, I did everything imaginable to act out and rebel. I was involved in many things that made my mother shudder with disbelief when I told her. As a young adult, I was careless with huge amounts of money and very self-destructive in my personal life. I lost my dad to alcohol-induced cirrhosis and my brother to a cocaine overdose all within the same year. My beautiful show horse died a gory death in front of my eyes and my first beloved dog drowned in a pool while I was standing nearby. These are all very horrible things, but I believe they were truly meant to be. I do not argue with them or my Creator. I believe these events helped shape me to be who I am. I believe these events help me coach clients, raise my kids, and support my husband. It is this belief that helps me live a life filled with joy and excitement in spite of and because of the things in my past.

I could have easily chosen to believe that I was unlucky. I could have chosen to believe that I was no good because of the situations I got myself involved with (you have no idea). But, I chose not to believe that I *was* my circumstance. I chose not to believe that I *was* my past or that I was doomed to repeat it. I chose to believe that I was meant to live a big wonderful life. So it is.

It's not the events in our lives that shape us, rather our beliefs about what those events mean. Generalizations about what we have learned guide all of our actions. Most of us do not decide consciously what we are going to believe. Often, beliefs are based on misinterpretations of past experiences. I have clients who believe they are damaged goods because they were molested or physically harmed. They live a life filled with arguing with the past and their perpetrator in their minds. They believe that if this event hadn't happened they would be happy and pure and innocent. I tell them that they already are pure and innocent and deserve to be happy despite what might have happened to them. I tell them that they can decide not to believe in the shame of the event. They can believe that they are glorious, not because of what did or didn't happen to them, but because they are a human, alive on the planet. I tell them that nothing can "take away" their essence. They believe something that isn't true. Just because you think you are damaged doesn't mean you are. You have the ability to believe that you are a whole, good, and magnificent person, who experienced something horrible. That horrible experience does not have the power to damage who you are at your core unless you believe it does and live your life as if it does.

Human beings have the power to hurt us physically. They have the power to overpower us emotionally as children. They can tell us to believe that we are wrong, horrible, shameful, and to blame. THEY CANNOT MAKE US BELIEVE THEM. As children, we can't make this distinction because we are still being taught what to believe. As adults, we can choose what we will and won't believe anymore. No matter what anyone says or does to us, we have the sacred, protected space of free will and choice over what we believe. No matter how big or powerful someone is, they cannot touch the space that determines what we believe. It is for us and for us alone. It is a sacred gift given to us by our Creator.

No matter what has happened to you. No matter if you were raped, molested, beaten, cheated, or rejected, you have the choice to believe what you want about the event and what it means to you. You have the choice of whether or not you are going to blame and believe your perpetrator or you can believe the truth: your soul is untouched by such harm unless you allow it. You can believe that no one can take your dignity, your hope, your self-love, or your joy without your permission. Even if someone takes your physical life, they cannot touch your soul.

Believe that you are worthy, gorgeous, wonderful, able, and strong, because you are. Believe that you have the power of the universe behind you and no human is a match for that. Believe that no matter how much fat you have on your body or how much pain you've had in your past, you can chose to believe that from this moment forward, you will believe in yourself. You will never believe anyone or anything that tries to tell you that you are less than glorious again!

Exercise:

* Make a list of all the negative beliefs you have that you are already aware of.

> *It's not what they did.*
> *It's what you believe about*
> *what they did that hurts.*

Belief Tool #2
We Have Many Illogical Beliefs
that Drive Us

A belief gives us a feeling of certainty about what things mean and who we are. If you want to know what your beliefs are, look at your life. Your life is your beliefs manifested. What we believe encompasses what we do, what we say, and how we react.

Anything you want to change in your life must be changed from the belief level if you want the change to be permanent. You cannot just treat the symptom; you must dig deep and get to the belief that caused you to get there in the first place.

For example, if you believe that you will always be overweight, it will be very difficult to lose weight permanently. Beliefs and reality like to be reflective of each other. When reality starts to contradict a belief, a tension is created in our life and this tension makes us uncomfortable. Many of us have no idea when this is happening; we just think we are stressed. At this point, we have two choices to reduce the tension: change the belief system or change the reality. Because most of us don't realize we have the negative belief, we have no choice but to sabotage our reality and gain our weight back in order to be back in line with what we believe.

This is a very common dance most of my clients experience. It's not until we get hold of the belief and change it that we find any permanent weight-loss results. It's very important to remember that many of the beliefs that drive us are completely illogical. When we discover the things we believe in, we might be tempted to disregard them because they seem so silly. This would be a very big mistake. Many of our belief systems were formed when we were small children and when we didn't have the emotional maturity to understand why things happen to us.

As children, we tend to blame ourselves for everything because we don't understand the complexities of other people's lives and experiences. We might believe that it's our fault if our parents fight all the time. We internalize the blame for the negative circumstances because the alternative of being completely out of control is unthinkable. We then believe that if we were better behaved, our parents wouldn't fight anymore. At least, we feel as if there is something we can do about it. We search for ways to cope and survive by trying to generalize what everything means. We take two unrelated things—our behavior and our parent's marriage—and we connect them. When our parents later divorce, we might internalize that and believe we were not good enough to keep them together.

The bad news is that many of us still have beliefs we developed when we were too young to know any better. We don't have a class in adulthood where someone comes in and reminds us that now we have the emotional maturity and tools to understand the realities of external circumstances. No one to remind us that there is now a way to question circumstances that have nothing to do with us—and not internalize them. We literally need to remind ourselves that we *are* good enough and that we always were. We need to go in and find all these old illogical beliefs and evaluate them with new eyes as adults.

Just because a belief seems illogical doesn't mean we still don't believe it.

The way we do this is by staying connected to ourselves and paying attention. When negative feelings come up and we feel them instead of denying them, they can be the doorway into our beliefs. For example, if you are feeling anxious because a man hasn't called, you can evaluate what is really going on deeper. You can think about what the real feeling is. It might start out as anxiety that makes you want to eat because there are no messages on your phone. If you sit with it and go deeper, you may see that you are really feeling fear. You can go deeper and see that you are afraid he won't call and that he will reject you. As you focus on this, you can see you are afraid of being rejected because, on some level, you don't think you are worthy of having a loving relationship. BINGO! Crappy belief system found. Maybe you didn't have much love from your dad when you were young so you started believing that you weren't worthy of a man's love. Here you are forty years later still believing it! Is it logical? No. But, on some level, you believe it to be true and it is causing you to have anxiety about him calling.

To further illustrate, imagine that you didn't have this belief. Imagine that you knew that you were worthy of deep, passionate, wondrous love. Imagine that you were solid in knowing how fabulous you are. Now, imagine coming home to no messages on the machine.

You don't jump to the belief that you will be rejected because it probably wouldn't occur to you. If, for some reason, this man rejected you, you would simply see that he was not the man for you. You would be able to look at it from a place of security and calmness because you believe you are worthy and you would know that you deserve love and that it is just going to be from yourself until the right man comes along.

Can you see how connected all this is to overeating and your weight? In the first belief, you might feel anxiety and overeat. You might even eat enough to gain weight. You then use the weight gain and the fact that you cannot fit into your clothes as further proof that you are not worthy of a loving relationship. With a lot of extra weight, you might attract fewer suitors, then further prove your belief systems to yourself. But it doesn't make it true! Just because you have found a way to prove to yourself that you are unworthy of love does not mean you are. It just means your belief system is being well fed, instead of evaluated and starved of proof.

So, to review. First, acknowledge and feel the feeling. Second, follow where it leads. When you get to the belief, pay attention to it no matter how illogical it might seem to you as an adult. See how it has manifested in your life. Then, get busy changing it to something true.

Exercise:

- Write down your most illogical belief—one you know you have but is not true. Now, write down its opposite. Is the opposite true? Why?

We believe our circumstances
are proof that our belief
is true, when it may be
the belief that is
manifesting our
circumstances.

Belief Tool #3
We Need to Change Belief Systems to Change Our Lives

My clients are always very eager to know exactly how to change their beliefs. They learn that they believe they will always be fat and they want to change the belief immediately. I tell them that they have spent much time proving their belief systems in their lives. They have gone out of their own way to make sure the belief is proved correct. The worst part about it is that they don't know they are doing it. I tell them that the way to get rid of a crappy belief system is to replace it with a good one and take action in their life to prove that one correct.

When we change the belief, it will feel awkward and new. We won't be convinced by it until we take it for a test drive and see how much better it makes us feel. When we start believing a new belief, sometimes many other illogical ones pop up around it. That is why we call it a belief system. Usually, there are many beliefs that are supporting each other. For example, if you believe you will always be overweight, it may be because you believe that you are weak, have no will power, that you are lazy, that life is hard, that you don't deserve success, that your metabolism is messed up, that you are ugly, and that it will always be a struggle. EUREKA. Belief system found. No wonder you are having a hard time losing weight. You are bumping up against all these beliefs that you actually believe.

One by one, we must dismantle this belief mess. None of these beliefs is true, and we need to stop believing them. How would you act if you didn't believe this system? How would your life be different? If all your actions were driven by the exact opposite of each of these beliefs, what results would you have and what would you feel? For example, if you believed you would end the weight struggle permanently within the next six months by losing all your excess weight permanently and you truly believed it, how would your life be different? If you believed you were strong, had amazing emotional control, that life could work with you instead of against you, that you deserved success beyond your wildest imagination, that your metabolism was perfect and it just needed you to align with it, and that you could truly be free of this for the rest of your life, what would your life look like? How would it be different than what it is today? What actions would be different? How would you feel on a daily basis?

> *The worst that can ever happen is a negative belief that things should be different than they are.*

The best way I know how to accomplish this is to act "as if." How would you act if you really believed this? If you really believed you were worthy, how would you act? Many times, my clients say they would feel less stressed, they wouldn't have to try so hard to make other people like them, they would go after the raise, they would talk to the guy, and they would start writing their book. What's better is they realize that if those things didn't work out, they would still know they were worthy. The event wouldn't cause them to change their mind.

As a coach, this is a very exciting process to watch. I am always filled with excitement when a client takes a risk and it doesn't turn out the way they wanted, but they come to the session and feel proud of themselves for having tried. The magical thing about this process is that it takes them to a place of power. If they believe that they will never struggle with their weight again and, for some reason, they gain a few pounds, they don't panic. They believe it won't be a struggle to lose it, and it isn't.

I use this quote from Wayne Dyer because I have never known anything to be truer. Read this aloud and let it really sink in:

"I will *see* it when I *believe* it."

Many of us choose to believe the opposite of this statement, but it is almost impossible to achieve something if you don't believe you can. You will constantly sabotage yourself to stay in line with your illogical system of beliefs. Change the belief first and then you can truly see it manifest in your life.

Exercise:

- What do you want to believe about yourself? Write down five beliefs you wish you had.

> You are going to believe something —why not believe something that helps you feel good?

Belief Tool #4
If You Don't Like What You Are Feeling, Change Your Belief

Any time you have a negative emotion you can question it. Why am I feeling sad? You might say, "I am sad because that man rejected me." Then, ask again, "Why does that make you sad?" You might then say something like, "It makes me sad because I am not attractive, lovable, or worthy of a man's love." HELLO! Belief System found! Now, we are really onto something.

The truth of the matter could be that the guy was gay, or intimidated because, perhaps, he thought he was out of his league; but you will never know because your negative belief system caused you to walk away when he didn't respond the way you wanted him to.

Whenever I find a belief system like this with a client, I jump up and down with excitement. (My client is usually in tears and despair at this moment.) "We found it!" I say. "Now, let's get rid of it." The genius author who taught me how to turn around belief systems is Byron Katie in her book *Loving What Is*. She is the master of this with her four-question turn around.

For each belief, she suggests asking these four questions: "Is it true? Can you absolutely know that it is true? How do you react when you think that thought? Who would you be without that thought?" I highly recommend all her books and her work. They have truly changed my life. I use a version of her technique with my clients when handling their negative beliefs.

I ask the client how they feel when they believe they are unlovable and not attractive. They usually say something like, "I feel awful and shy and I feel like I want to hide" (now there's a good way to attract a man). I ask them how they act. They usually say that they act cold and aloof in order to not risk rejection.

It's at this point that I say, "Do you think maybe he didn't respond to you because you were being cold and not because you are unattractive?" Hmmm. Maybe. Maybe? I bet you could bank on it.

I then ask my client, "If you were to get rid of this belief system, how would you feel?"

The answer invariably comes back with, "Happy, fun, outgoing, and excited." I don't need to tell you from which place you will be more attractive to the opposite sex.

It is fascinating to me how much we can control our feelings by what we believe. Anytime I am feeling something negative, I see it as an opportunity to discover some negative belief that is lurking within me. I actually look forward to these feelings coming so I can get access to myself and change myself for the better.

For example, last week I was frustrated with my assistant, Angela, because she didn't complete a job in a timely manner and in the way I had asked her to complete it. Now, in this situation many would say I had a "right" and that I was "justified" for feeling this way. Although that might be true, I did not want to feel frustrated. I do not see an upside to feeling frustrated or reacting to frustration. So, I let frustration come up and swim around without me reacting to it. I let it lead me to the belief system that was causing it. What I found was very interesting. I found that I had a belief system that indicated that if my assistant didn't produce the assignment on time, that I would disappoint my client and that I would appear unprofessional and lacking. Fascinating. I looked at that belief and found that it was completely untrue. If my client believed that about me, it was still untrue. Further, I realized that I have no control over what my client believes and I was actually trying to control her feelings by my actions. I took it deeper and asked myself what I thought it meant if my client saw me as unprofessional. What I found was a belief system that told me that I was not capable. I knew that this was completely illogical and I was able to turn it around immediately.

The best part about it is that I was able to talk to my assistant free from emotions caused by illogical belief systems. I was able to communicate to her that the work was unacceptable without reacting and shaming her with my own frustration. In essence, I was able to maintain my professionalism and see that I was capable of handling the situation well. It was the exact opposite of what my illogical belief system would have had me do.

By changing my belief, I was able to change my feelings immediately. I didn't deny that I was feeling frustrated but used it as a tool. In the old days, I might have yelled at Angela, then gone to the kitchen and

---

Beliefs cause feelings, which cause actions, which cause results. If you change the belief—you ultimately change the results.

---

eaten a frozen pizza all in an attempt to avoid looking at the belief that I am not capable. Now, with the tools I have, I can go into a belief system and prove it wrong in a matter of minutes without gaining any weight.

Exercise:

- Think of something that you believe causes you to have a negative feeling. Ask yourself why you feel negative. Keep asking why until you find the belief.

- I am upset. Why? Because my jeans don't fit. Why? Because I ate so much this week. Why? *Because I have no willpower and I am weak.* This is the belief system to challenge.

I always am saying "I don't know" is not an acceptable answer.

You do know.

Go – and find your answers.

Belief Tool #5
Believing that You Are Internally Rather than Externally Controlled

This is where I break rank with many of my colleagues. So many of the weight-control books I read are filled with suggestions for controlling the external environment. They recommend, for example, taking all the junk food out of your house, removing the bread basket from the table, not attending parties where you know you'll be tempted, and avoiding people who cause you to feel anxiety.

I say bring in the junk food and bring in the people. I am always telling my clients that I want them to be sitting at a buffet with all their favorite junk food, experiencing the worst day of their life, surrounded by people who drive them crazy and to be *internally controlled*. I want them to have the freedom and confidence that comes from the emotional work within, not from controlling the environment or other people. I actually encourage my clients to put themselves in tempting situations and let the feelings come up. It is a wonderful tool to get access to belief systems. Eventually, you get to the place of freedom where nothing can tempt you to dishonor yourself and your commitments.

There are always going to be events and circumstances you cannot control. Parties happen. Holidays happen. If you avoid these situations because you believe you don't have the internal control to manage them, you are actually proving your negative belief system right and letting it run you. If you keep the junk food in your house and use it as a way to feel, instead of eat, then you get access and you can change the belief forever. That is how this works permanently. The strength is created within.

For example, you are sitting at home, watching TV, and you have an urge to eat the bag of potato chips in the pantry. Instead of fighting the urge, getting anxious, and eating the whole bag, try feeling what the urge feels like. Explore it. Why are you having the urge? Many of my clients realize they are having the urge as a reaction to another feeling and their desire to distract them from it. Maybe they are feeling bored and the urge to eat potato chips offers the excitement of the drama of overeating and judgment. Okay, stay with the boredom. What does that feel like? Go deeper. You might find that boredom is coming up because your kids are at camp and you would usually be with them right now. Then, you access loneliness. Then, you might access the belief that without being a mom to your kids, you are worthless and lazy and all you do is watch TV. There it is. Negative belief. Not true.

From here, you can explore who you are besides a mom. You can get to know some of your dreams that have nothing to do with being a parent. You can realize that you believe you are an amazing writer who hasn't been writing because you believe you are only a mom. Then, you can turn it around and start believing you can be a mom and a writer. You can turn off the TV and start writing. Excitement and joy can now fill your body based on your new belief that is empowering. Potato chips? What potato chips? I am not hungry.

The other area where I disagree with many of my colleagues is an old concept in psychology and in coaching that talks about identifying, then getting our needs met, by telling our loved ones what they can do to meet our needs. I do not agree with this technique at all because it makes you completely dependent on other people to meet your needs. For example, if I don't feel loved in my life, this philosophy says that I should tell my husband about it, then give him ideas on how he can make me feel more loved. Maybe I could suggest he buy me flowers, hug me more, or light candles in the bedroom. The belief is that if my husband does these things then I will feel more love from him. All I can say is *pahleeese!*

There is nothing fun about anyone in your life telling you how to behave in order to make *them* happy. "You need to call me back when I call you or it hurts my feelings." No. How about you just don't get your feelings hurt and not leave your feelings up to how *I* behave? How about just loving others for who they are? Now that is a fun place to be. Being with someone who has no expectations of how you should behave and just loves you for who you are—MAKES IT EASY TO GIVE. I always want to give to my husband because he doesn't expect it and he always appreciates it. It makes it fun to give. If he handed me a manual on how to meet his needs, I would feel resentful and angry—not to mention out of control of my own life.

Anytime your joy is dependent on someone else, you are going to be disappointed. It's never someone else's job to meet your needs (unless you are a small dependent child, who many of us still believe we are). It's YOUR job to meet your own needs. If you need more love, give it to yourself; if you feel empty, fill yourself up. Light yourself some candles, buy yourself some flowers, and say sweet nothings into your own ear. Your marriage isn't suffering because your husband is acting or not acting in a certain way. You *believe* your marriage is suffering because your husband isn't following the manual you so lovingly supplied him with.

> *If your happiness depends on what someone else does or doesn't do, you are going to be unhappy a lot of the time.*

So many of my clients tell me they feel desperate and trapped. When I ask them to follow the feeling to their belief system, they inevitably follow it to their husband, their job, or their kids. They tell me that if their husband was kinder and more attentive and their kids were better behaved and their job was less stressful then they would feel better. Client after client tells me that she would be happier if her husband showed her more attention. HELLO! You aren't giving yourself the time of day; you are ignoring your basic emotional and physical health and you want your husband to pay more attention to you? YOU FIRST!

You teach people how to treat you. If you aren't treating yourself with kindness and love, please don't expect anyone else to do it for you instead; you have shown them that you don't think you deserve it.

I suggest they skip the middle-man and just feel better. When you believe your emotional happiness is dependent on how others act, you will constantly try to control how they act and what they say and what kind of grade they get and how often they praise you. As many of you know, this can be quite exhausting. IT NEVER WORKS. No one can make you feel anything. You can have the best looking life in the world and still feel awful. You can be at your goal weight and still feel fat.

It is not the circumstance or the person that you need to control. It is what you believe about yourself and what you believe about the events that you need to control. Everything you need for your own happiness is within you now at this very moment. You don't have to do anything but control your own belief systems to feel good right this minute. In fact, if you truly believed you were happy, you would be. Even if your husband didn't tell you how fabulous you are.

The truth is that neediness is not fun. If you "need" your husband to tell you how attractive you are, it makes you less so. If I tell my husband I *need* him to call twice a day it makes him less likely to do it out of love. If I tell my husband he has to buy me a romantic gift so I can feel good, he feels resentful not romantic. We can actually deter the exact thing we most desire. When people genuinely love themselves, they do not go looking for someone else to do it for them. They take responsibility for it. What is most amazing about this is that when you take responsibility for your own love, you will attract so much other love into your life. Two people who really love themselves can get together and be free of the burden of filling the other person up. Freedom in a loving relationship is a good time. You are already full of love for yourself, so anything your partner gives you is not "needed," and actually just a bonus. It will just be gravy on an already amazing sense of fullness. You will be full, and others will want to be around you because you aren't grabbing and wanting.

Exercise:

- Make a list of your needs.
- Next to each need write how you can fulfill that need yourself without relying on someone else.

There is nothing another person has that you need. Everything you need is within you now.

Belief Tool #6
Beliefs Are Choices

We really decide what is true in our own lives. We might as well choose to believe the truth. The truth is that we are all filled with an abundant source of love. The truth is that each one of us has a place on the planet that is ours to inhabit and shine. The truth is we have free will and control of our emotional lives. We can decide to acknowledge and live this truth. We can make a choice that we are no longer willing to be defined by our old, outdated belief systems and we choose to believe that we are loved. By living our truth, we can stop stuffing it with food.

You are truly amazing. This is not an arrogant concept at all. I am not suggesting that you are any more amazing than anyone else on the planet, just that you realize you are equally as amazing as each other divinely created being. We all have an equal ability to be whom we are meant to be. I know for sure that we are not meant to believe lies about how inadequate or unloved we are. We are loved beyond our wildest imaginations. We have the ability to tap into that love by choosing to honor and love ourselves. When we do that, our ability to give love is increased dramatically.

Choose to believe that you are worthy of all the blessings this world has to offer, and then see the manifestation of this in your own life before your own eyes. I believe that you can lose the weight. I believe that you can be free from the struggle. I believe that you are beautiful and wonderful. I believe you have what it takes to make all your dreams come true.

What do you chose to believe? I have listed below many of the belief systems that my clients have had in the past before they began this process. They are all untrue, but very powerful if believed. Please review the following list and note any that you might currently have.

- I am not worthy of attention.
- I am not normal.
- I am not loved.
- I am ugly.
- I will never be attractive.
- I will never have companionship.
- I have no will power.
- I am weak.
- I am a failure.
- I am alone.
- I am defective.
- I am not a priority.
- Everyone else is more important.
- I can't get my needs met.

- *I will never lose weight.*
- *I will always struggle.*
- *I will always have to carefully watch my weight.*

Let's turn each one around, and then go about proving them true by taking action in our own lives:

- *I am worthy of my own attention.*
- *I am extraordinary.*
- *I am loved deeply by my Creator and myself.*
- *I am gorgeous.*
- *I am attractive.*
- *I provide myself with wonderful companionship.*
- *I have the will to be powerful in my life.*
- *I am strong.*
- *I am a survivor.*
- *I am never alone; I am connected to the universe.*
- *I am perfect in my existence—exactly the way I am meant to be right now.*
- *I am my #1 priority.*
- *Everyone else is important, but I must fill myself up first before I can give it away.*
- *I can meet my own needs.*
- *I can work with my body and my life instead of against it.*
- *I will be free of this weight struggle once and for all so I can put my emotional energy into more purposeful things.*

To access more belief systems, I have my clients stand on the scale. (I hear you gasping.) So many of my colleagues recommend you throw your scale away. I think it is a button that can bring up emotion and negative belief systems that need to be replaced. It is a wonderful external trigger for learning. Use the following Hello Scale Worksheet to evaluate your belief about what the number on the scale means. Let all the emotions and crappy belief systems surface and then write them down. Obviously, the number on the scale is an external circumstance that you are allowing to define you. What you believe is true about a number on a scale can change who you decide to be.

When you believe a piece of metal (a scale) has the power to make you feel happy or sad, you are confused. It is your story about what that number means causing the emotion.

Hello Scale Worksheet

Number today: *(e.g. 250)* _____

1. How do I choose to feel about this number? *(e.g., angry)*

_____

_____

_____

_____

2. What do I believe this number means? *(e.g., that I am going to be fat for the rest of my life)*

_____

_____

_____

_____

3. What is the truth? *(e.g., I do not have to always weigh 250, I have the power to change my weight)*

_____

_____

_____

_____

4. Could I peacefully own this number as a fact and not a statement about my life? *(e.g., Yes. I happen to weight 250 right now, but this is not an indicator of anything to do with the rest of my life)*

_____

_____

_____

_____

5. Describe what it feels like factually and without judgement to be in a body that weighs this number. *(e.g., uncomfortable, tired, bigger than others)*

_____

_____

_____

_____

6. What can I choose to believe that is empowering ? *(e.g., This is my starting point and I will lose this weight permanently this time and never weigh 250 again—I am capable of changing this reality)*

_____

_____

_____

_____

7. What can I do to prove this belief system true? *(e.g., Eat on the hunger scale, be willing to feel my feelings instead of eating)*

_____

_____

_____

_____

_____

Review of how to use the eating and belief system tools when you feel like overeating:

1. Urge to overeat.
2. Remind yourself that you do not want to eat/overeat right now.
3. Ask: What am I feeling now?
4. Surface emotions may be anxiety or stress.
5. Relax into theses surface emotions until they pass.
6. Ask: What am I feeling deeper?
7. Feel that feeling through.
8. Ask: Why am I feeling this feeling?
9. Keep asking why until you get to the belief.
10. Evaluate the belief.
11. Change the belief.
12. Prove the new one right.
13. How would you feel if you really believed the new belief?
14. Act as if.

Example:

1. Urge to eat.
2. Remind myself I don't want to eat now because I am not hungry.
3. What am I feeling? Anxiety.
4. Feel the anxiety and let it be in my body.
5. What's under the anxiety? Anger.

6. Why? Because I am mad I can't have it.
7. Why? Because I never get what I want.
8. Why? Because I am unlucky and fat.
9. Take all three of these belief systems and turn them around.

    I can have it, I just choose not to.

    I can have anything I truly want that adds value to my life.

    I create my own luck.

    I don't ever have to react to my feelings, I can just sit and feel them.

10. Don't eat—prove new belief right. Think about what it is I truly want for myself right now.
11. I feel free and in control. I feel empowered.
12. Urge dissapated.
13. Repeat if needed.

When you have an urge
to eat when you're not hungry,
it's time to get to know yourself.

Make Yourself Proud by Taking Care

"No one can take away your pride."

Self-Care Tool #1
Make You the Number One Priority in Your Life

I cannot count the number of times I have heard clients say they don't have enough time to plan meals, feel their feelings, or exercise. It's a tragedy. All of these well-meaning women give so much to everyone else, but leave the scraps to themselves. I tell them all the same thing: you can't pour love from an empty pitcher.

The hardest part of this scenario is that giving to others at your expense can be externally rewarding. You are viewed as a giver and you really are; but inside, you are starving for your own attention. I think this is one of the reasons we become overweight; we are trying to get our own attention. The most important person to take care of is you. Period. If you aren't healthy, you won't be any good to anyone. Also, for those of you who have kids: You need to remember the best legacy you can give to your kids is an example of a life well-lived. They may listen to what you say, but they will do what you do. If you tell them to take care of themselves and you don't do it yourself, what kind of message are you sending?

You must become number one. You do not ever sacrifice healthy eating, exercise, or your emotional health for the sake of anyone else...ever. If someone really needs you, they need you to be healthy and available. Put your own oxygen mask on first and then take care of the kids or anyone else who needs you. The ironic part of this process is that once you start taking care of yourself, you have so much more to give to others. It doesn't take away from them; it adds value and joy to their lives. So grab that to-do list and make sure you are at the top of it every time!

I am sure you have heard this advice before and understood it intellectually, but now it is time to start applying this practice. I am very extreme with this advice and I require my clients to at least try it out. What this means is that (sometimes) the kids have to give up on some of their activities so mom can have one of her own. This means that friends don't always get the help they need and dinner is not quite ready at the exact time expected. This is very difficult for many women. I have had one client in tears when she told her family they would have to wait twenty minutes to leave for the amusement park because she wanted to get her exercise in. Her family was shocked by the request. They were used to her dropping everything so the family could be happy. She had taught them that her need to take care of herself wasn't important. She should have expected them to be shocked when she showed them a new way to treat her by treating her workout as important.

Another common situation I hear from my clients is that there was a special circumstance that made it impossible to have fuel food ready or time to workout. When I inquire about the situation, it is usually a party they were throwing for someone or a PTA meeting or a son's basketball tournament. The truth is that there will always be these things vying for your attention. My answer is that those things are all secondary to your emotional health and physical care. If you can't take care of yourself and throw a party, cancel the party. If you can't work out and attend your son's tournament, you don't see your son play. Almost 100 percent of the time, my clients find a way to do both; if they can't, I insist they put themselves first. I can hear the complaints from you reading this as clearly as I hear my clients. This seems extreme to them and out of the ordinary. I assure you it isn't. It is one of the most important actions you can take to make this program work for you.

Exercise:

- Make a list of your top ten priorities. Make sure your health and well-being are at the top.

1. _____

2. _____

3. _____

4. _____

5. _____

6. _____

7. _____

8. _____

9. _____

10. _____

Self-Care Tool #2
Not Taking Care of Yourself Is Procrastination of Your Work in the World

Often, when I am coaching on this subject, my clients will describe their self-sacrifice as a noble thing. In many ways, some minor sacrifices are necessary to give to your family, as well as to your job, etc. But it's NEVER noble to sacrifice your health in any way for anyone. One of your responsibilities on the planet is to work through your emotional roadblocks. Distracting yourself *from* yourself in order to handle the problems of everyone else is a cop-out. It's the way you procrastinate the work of your *own* life. It's YOUR RESPONSIBILITY as a mature adult to clean out your emotional closet and take care of yourself physically on a regular basis. You cannot convince me that other people's needs can be dealt with at the expense of your own...ever.

I know it might sound harsh. I know it might sound like I am not giving you credit for all it is you do for your family or your job. I am never impressed when the sacrifice is obviously taking the toll on the giver and the giver acts like they don't have a choice. They believe that they are doing the right thing by sacrificing their dreams, goals, and needs for the sake of their family. There are many groups of people who believe family values means we must give up our immediate desires in order to take good care of our families. I have heard them argue on the radio that America is going to hell in a hand basket because parents are so into their own dreams that they lose track of their family values and family meaning. I respectfully disagree with this assumption. I see more women who are giving up all their needs and throwing themselves into their family with no regard to themselves. There is a balance and it is not found in self-sacrifice. It is found in loving our families from a place of self-care. It is through paying attention to ourselves and growing ourselves that we set an example for our kids. Being a good parent is about being your best, and not just attending sports activities or being available to drive them everywhere. Having self-value is the starting point where you can begin to teach your family values.

---

*Taking care of yourself
is never selfish.*

I can hear you, "But, you don't know my schedule. I have four kids; I can't possibly find time to workout." Or, "I work full time as a therapist and I see ten clients a day. There is no way I can find the time to plan healthy fuel meals and eat when I am hungry." Then quit. Then take the kids outside and have them watch you run or walk or ride your bike. I understand your schedule, and I understand that your business and your family are important. I understand that life is busy and everyone needs you. But, you need you. By putting yourself last, you are ignoring your true work on this planet. You are not going in and getting to know yourself and becoming who you are meant to be in every role in your life. It is your job to develop yourself and keep growing. Stop procrastinating and get to work on yourself.

Exercise:

- Write down the reasons you have put other people before yourself.
- How do these reasons make you feel?

You need you.

Self-Care Tool #3
Be Good Company

You are stuck with yourself for the rest of your life. Is this a good thought or a dreadful one? Do you like to hang out with yourself? Are you nice and wonderful and sweet to yourself? Many times, we think we want our husband or significant other to be more of something. I hear it all the time. "If he would just pay more attention to me." What about you? How much attention are you giving yourself? You want him to be more considerate in the way he talks to you, but how do you talk to yourself?

Being with someone (you) who says to you all day:

- You are fat.
- You are ugly.
- What is wrong with you?
- I don't like you.
- You have no willpower.
- You are disgusting.
- Gosh, you're dumb.
- Get your act together.
- You are so lazy.
- You will never be thin.

THIS IS NOT SOMEONE YOU SHOULD WANT TO SPEND TIME WITH!

Wouldn't it be wonderful to have someone in your life who adored you all the time and told you how wonderful you are on a regular basis? You can! You can feel joy by remembering how wonderful *you* are. You won't *need* anyone else to tell you because you are telling it to yourself every day. Some of us don't acknowledge ourselves and forget that our Creator doesn't make anything less than fabulous.

Don't wait for compliments. Give them to yourself. **Learn the skill of creating your own joy.** Give yourself some credit for everything you have done to survive. Acknowledge yourself for reading a book in hopes of helping yourself grow.

I often tell my clients to give themselves a standing ovation for getting out of bed in the morning (wouldn't that be cool?). After you complete a successful shower, give yourself a pat on the back. Sounds cheesy and corny? What's the alternative? Dragging your ass out of bed and looking in the mirror and saying, "Yuck?" No thanks.

Don't make up affirmations that you don't believe in or try to convince yourself that you are something you are not. It's not necessary. Just look for the things you really do like about *you*. When I ask my clients to make a list of things they like about themselves, they think it's going to be difficult, then they are surprised to see how many things they really do appreciate about who they are. "Well, I do have nice eyes...and I guess I am a good friend...and I work hard at my job"...etc.

That's what we want to celebrate: the truth about you. No B.S. or flashing lights of exaggeration. You don't need it. There is plenty that is wonderful right there in the truth.

In the moments when you are alone with yourself, you should savor the truth about yourself. I am always surprised when people tell me they don't want to do things alone. I love being alone. It gives me time to reflect and connect with myself. I can give myself credit for what I have done well and I can allow myself to be filled with gratitude for all the joy I have in my life. I can genuinely have a good time hanging out with myself for an entire weekend, no problem. I am very good company to myself. If you think being alone is lonely, it is because you are not paying attention to yourself. If being alone makes you feel bored, it might be because you are acting boring. Talk to yourself in a wonderful way, find out what you love to do and then do it. Be great company to yourself, then when other people come, it just adds to the party.

Exercise:

- Make a list of the things you genuinely like about yourself.

It is not arrogant to like yourself.

Liking who you are is not about taking credit for being fabulous.

It is just noticing and appreciating that you are by design and you are not the designer.

Self-Care Tool #4
Give Yourself a Time Out
for Being Mean

I have a pre-work questionnaire that I have all my clients fill out before I'll start coaching them. On it, I ask them to describe themselves and how they look physically. You may not be surprised to hear that the descriptions are filled with judgment and cruel words. "I have an ugly face and a disgusting stomach." Or, "My butt is so huge and gross I am afraid to walk outside." Would you ever allow someone to speak to you this way? Would you allow your child to speak to a friend in this manner? No way.

We are always disciplining little kids when they are mean to each other. Now, it's your turn. My clients know that if they are going to be mean to themselves, they are required to put themselves in a time out. It is really time to put your foot down with yourself. Any time you catch yourself being mean or saying something that is unkind, stop immediately. Let yourself know this kind of talk is not acceptable. Being mean will NOT be tolerated anymore. It stops today. As of this moment, everything negative you say to yourself needs to change.

There is not one good reason you can give me for being mean to yourself. There is no upside. It creates dejection and insecurity, which are the last things we need. So stop it! Stop it! Stop it! Never again are you allowed to say anything that isn't supportive or wonderful. If you do, take five.

I know it sounds juvenile and basic and it is. But, this is a very powerful tool. Many of us have no idea how often we are negative with ourselves on a daily basis. We usually aren't paying close attention, but when we start to take notice, it can be surprising what we have been living with. If you pay attention to your thoughts throughout your day, you can note the ones that are mean and unacceptable. Pay attention like you are a strict third grade teacher and don't be shy in handing out the reminders.

Exercise:

• Write down the negative things you say to yourself and ways you are mean to yourself. Make a commitment to stop right now.

> *There is never an upside to being mean to yourself.*

Self-Care Tool #5
Be a Compassionate Observer

My best asset as a coach is perspective. It is very easy for me to see the issues in my clients' lives with clarity because I am not "in" their lives. I try to help my clients step out of their lives and look at themselves with a new perspective. I tell them to come sit with me and look at them and tell me what they think is going on. It is very powerful. It helps separate the activities of life from the person living it. I require they maintain compassion when they are doing this, and I have them observe themselves with love and not judgment.

Understand that you will make mistakes. You will blow it and do things that are just plain awful. So what? This is not a good time to start beating yourself up; this is a good time to try to understand what is going on with you. Start questioning why you do things, give yourself the benefit of the doubt, and realize that you have a very good reason for doing it. You can *dislike* something you've done and still like yourself.

This is a very powerful tool when feelings seem too overwhelming to feel. Sometimes, we can't seem to find the feeling or relax enough to let it come up. If we allow ourselves to become the compassionate observer of what we are doing and what we are feeling, we can be removed enough to see what might be really going on. See yourself from the part of you that is unchanging and unaffected by the world. See how things play out without berating yourself.

When I am doing this personally, it helps me to think of myself out of my body, looking down on myself and watching. It is like the scene from so many movies I have seen when someone is dying and they are above themselves, watching themselves die from a different perspective. Once I am able to visualize myself outside of my body looking down, I can understand, with much love, why I might want to overeat or be frustrated. I am able to get clarity much faster on what I am feeling and why. I can locate the belief system and notice it without actually believing it; from here I can decide to change it.

As the observer, you look at everything that is happening without taking any of it personally. You are able to look at what you do and what happens to you from a perspective of "fascinating" and "interesting" without making judgments that it shouldn't or should be happening. It is what it is and you are just compassionately noticing what it is. It is almost a quiet sense of knowing that reality is exactly what reality is supposed to be. It feels free and light. There is no argument against it. There is no negative emotion about it. It just is.

Many people think this might put you into a place where you won't take action. By finding acceptance, you won't try to make anything better or change anything. The opposite is actually true. Instead of fighting reality, you can accept reality and work with it instead of against it. You can acknowledge what you believe to be true, and from there, you can change it. It doesn't need to feel forced or contrived. It is like yielding and moving into line with life so you can direct yourself to your dreams.

So many times clients tell me they were bad because they ate a cookie or they shouldn't have skipped an exercise. I tell them to look at the situation from the compassionate-observer perspective. What is going on there? From this perspective, they can take out the judgment and understand that they ate due to a belief that they were unloved and that it's okay. From here, we can turn that belief around. They can notice that they didn't work out because they felt it would be selfish to make the time for themselves. Interesting. From here, they can change that belief and decide to believe they are worth the time. The compassionate observer can see there is a reason for all things and they don't require judgment, only compassion. When we come from a place of compassion, change can be gentle and permanent. Your compassionate witness is ALWAYS compassionate and never judging, no matter what it is you or anyone else has done.

Exercise:

- As you read this, become the observer watching yourself read. As a *compassionate* observer, what do you notice about yourself?

When I am compassionately observing myself, I look at every action I take and say "Of course I did that," it helps everything make sense.

Self-Care Tool #6
Do What You Genuinely Want Long-Term, Not What You Feel Like Doing Right Now

When you are first replacing belief systems, it's often necessary to separate what you "feel like" from what you "really want." Feelings, at this point, may be stemming from the negative belief systems. So, even though you need to acknowledge them, you don't always want to react to them at this point. Instead, you must decide what you really want and why.

For example, one afternoon you *feel like* sitting on the couch and not going into the gym. You just feel like relaxing. (This feeling may be coming from a belief that you are lazy.) It's at this point you have to remember why you *want* to exercise. Bring up all the reasons and remember that you want to work out even though you don't feel like it. Don't confuse how you feel in the moment with what you want in the moment. In this way, you aren't doing something you don't want to do, so there is no forcing anything. You just acknowledge that you are feeling low on energy, but you want to work out to achieve a greater goal. Then, you go and get it done.

In many instances, we let our feelings run the show and what we want gets pushed away. Most of us have no idea this is even happening. We want to write a book, but we feel like watching TV. We want to work out, but we feel like running an errand. It is important to notice and feel your feelings and then make the decision to do what you want. You need to let your feelings know they will be acknowledged, but not obeyed. Feelings that are coming from negative belief systems are wonderful because they lead us to the belief system, but we can't let them lead our lives.

After you start living from a place of what you want versus what you feel like, you gain control and your life starts reflecting your true desires and your new beliefs that are healthy and supportive to you. Each time you do something to prove your new belief correct, you diminish the disempowering belief. Eventually, what you feel will be the same as what you want. In the meantime, there is an uncomfortable transition of overriding "feel like" for a while.

One of my amazing clients learned this lesson early in her coaching and it completely changed her life. She had a very messy house that she couldn't keep clean and a body that was carrying about one hundred pounds of extra weight. When we set minimum baselines for walking three times a week and she would come to the session saying she hadn't done it, I would ask her, "Why?" She would say that she hadn't felt like it. She would say it in a way as if to state that was a very strong, legitimate reason. She had not learned the tool of noticing what she *felt* like doing, then deciding to do what she *wanted* to do despite her negative feelings. I suggested that she do what she wants and not what she feels like. I told her I thought she was letting negative feelings that originated from negative beliefs run her life without her permission. She was flabbergasted at this perspective and decided to give it a try. She hasn't missed a workout since. Amazingly, those feelings of not wanting to work out at some point disappeared. She is strong in her confidence of what she wants in her life, and she knows if those feelings come back, she will feel them, and then do what she *wants* to do anyway.

This is one of the best ways I know to build self-confidence and pride. When things come easy to us, we don't feel as proud as when they are more difficult. The act of acknowledging that something is difficult because we don't feel like doing it and then doing it anyway for ourselves is a deposit into our own emotional bank account. As we do this over and over out of self-love, meeting our own needs to achieve our dreams, self-pride grows. Self-pride is a gift that must be earned and can't ever be taken away, and it tastes sweeter than any piece of chocolate cake I have ever tried.

Exercise:

- Write down something you want to do but haven't done because you haven't felt like it.
- How does it feel to know you have obeyed a feeling over true desire?
- Is it shocking to see that your feelings have been running your life?

When clients tell me they don't
want to do something hard,
I disagree.
I tell them that accomplishing
something that was hard
is one of the best feelings
in the world.
Most of the time they end up
agreeing, once it is done.

Self-Care Tool #7
Diversify Your Joy

One of the first questions I ask most clients is how much of their total joy in life comes from food and food-related activities. When the percentage is high, I understand why they are having a hard time losing weight. I had one client, mentioned earlier in this book, who lived alone and didn't have much outside interaction. Of all the joy she had in her life, 95 percent came from food. As you can imagine, she was not too excited to reduce her food intake as it was directly connected to the amount of joy she would experience in her life.

Whenever this is the case, I don't start with the food, I start with the joy. I didn't attempt to have the client reduce her food intake until she added at least 50 percent more joy from other sources into her life. In this particular client's case, she made a list of all the things in her life she could start doing that could bring her more joy. She learned how to fish, she took a jewelry-making class, she started walking, she spent more time with her friends, and she joined a volunteer organization. All of these activities started to fill her with joy and happiness and a sense of contribution. At this point, it was easier for her to stop overeating because she could rely on herself for her joy instead of just the food.

A good rule of thumb is if you feel like you need more than 10 percent joy food per day you are most likely getting too much of your joy from food. If you feel as if you are really missing out on something when you can't eat 50 percent or more joy food, that is an indication that your joy needs to be diversified from food into other activities and practices that can help you create happiness.

If it isn't food you are getting joy from, you still don't want to have all your joy in one basket. If it's all wrapped up in a man, when the man leaves, you can be devastated. If a huge percentage of joy comes from your kids, then when they leave, you are left feeling empty. If you get most of your joy from your work, when you quit or get fired or end your career, you can be left feeling unhappy. So spread out the joy in your life. Use all the balanced sources in life from your family, your career, your social life, and your spiritual life so they can work together in bringing you a steady sense of well-diversified joy.

As I discussed earlier, there is a tremendous amount of joy that can come from within. We are connected to the universe in ways we can hardly understand. When we are truly connected to ourselves, we can be connected to all that is love, joy, and excitement. We can decide we deserve our own love and take steps to find things that fill us with a sense of wonder and happiness.

Exercise:

- Write down your top five sources of joy.
- Is one much more heavily weighted than the others?
- Is there one you would like to reduce? Increase?

Enjoying food is only one
of many joys in life.

Find your other sources of joy.

Self-Care Tool #8
Don't Worship "Busy"

If I had a nickel for every time someone used the excuse that they were too busy, I would be a very wealthy woman. Do yourself a favor and don't ever use that as a reason for not doing anything ever again. "Busy" is the generalized excuse we use for not going after our dreams. It is the ultimate dream stealer. It is important to remember that we define our busy. We are the ones who choose what we will do with our time and our day. We create this state for ourselves. It is important to look at it regularly and question it and decide if it is how we want to live.

Instead of saying that I was too busy to work out say, "I chose to lie on the couch and watch TV instead of working out." Or, "I chose to see my daughter's play instead of going for a walk." Everything you do in your life is a choice, even if it doesn't feel like it. You choose to go to work, you choose to take care of your family, and you can choose to take care of yourself. "Busy" is a dark hole of vagueness that will never help you get a handle on anything. Be specific so you can identify what it is in your life that is and isn't working. Kick "busy" to the curb.

I had a client who was a high-level executive who was too busy to do anything she really wanted. I asked her immediately to define busy for me. She went on to describe her day of running errands, going to meetings, picking up her kids, going to the store, making dinner, doing laundry, and answering client's calls. She had lumped these activities into a seemingly unchangeable busy. Busy was living her life and it was at the expense of what she really wanted. I suggested she change her plan by writing down everything that was important to her and putting that at the top of the list and then adding activities from the busy pile under that. At first, she thought it would be impossible to add one more thing to her day. On evaluating how she was spending her time, she saw ways she could delegate and eliminate some of her busy. It really worked. She had the mantra, "Me first, busy second." The ultimate result was that she was able to fulfill her own needs and actually handle the rest with much more peace because she saw it as a choice, not a forced reality of life.

Don't confuse "being busy"
with living your life.

One of the best secrets to eliminating busy from our lives to is learn how to say "no." Many times, we say "yes" when we want to say "no." We go to parties and functions we don't want to attend and we eat food we don't want to eat. I love how Oprah says that NO is a complete sentence. When should you say no? Whenever it's the truth. Living a life that is based on truth is freeing and wonderful. You eat when you are truly hungry, you spend time with people you truly like, and you live a life you truly want.

I have heard it said many times that fat and the truth do not mix. I think this may be one of the most important tools in this book to learn. When you begin to tell the truth about your real hungers and real emotions, you can begin to live *your truth*. The truth really does set you free. Sometimes, the truth sounds like this: "No."

Exercise:

1. Define your busy. When you say you have been busy, what does that include doing?
2. Are all of these things necessary? Are all these things wants?

Self-Care Tool #9
Ask a Great Question Every Day

We all ask ourselves questions all day long, "How can I get this done?" "What am I going to eat today?" "When will I be skinny?" "Why is my life is so hard?" In coaching, questions are the tools we use to change our lives. By asking high-quality, empowering questions, we get creative and inspiring answers. It is like your brain goes to work searching for the answers to what you are presenting. If you ask, "How can I be happier?" your brain comes back with wonderful ideas. If you don't close the door with answering, "I don't know," you will find a source of wisdom within you that you might not have known existed. The higher quality the question, the higher quality the answer will be.

If you ask yourself why you can't lose weight, you will come back with a slew of very negative self-defeating answers. You have incorporated a negative belief into the question and your brain will be sent to task to prove the negative belief correct. Your brain is a very powerful tool that is able to do just that. It may come back with: "You don't have willpower, you don't have enough time, you don't care enough." But, if you change the question to incorporate an empowering belief, you will come up with answers that are just as empowering. For example, it could change to: "How can I lose weight permanently and have fun at the same time?" You will likely come up with much more creative and wonderful ideas that will move you closer toward your goal.

So, take a moment right now and see if you can identify the questions you ask yourself on a regular basis. You might even have one main one about your weight that you want to evaluate. My main question for a long time was, "Why does keeping my weight down have to be such a struggle for the rest of my life?" One day, my brain came back with, "It doesn't." I changed my question to, "How can I end this struggle permanently and without deprivation or pain?" Suddenly I began to get the answers that are found throughout this book. Whatever your question is, decide if it is empowering and if it isn't, change it immediately. Write it on a Post-It and put it up everywhere in your house. Your brain will go to work for you and most likely come up with a wonderful solution.

My current question is: "How can I be an example of what is possible?"

Pick one question to ask yourself every day. Here are some ideas if you need some help:

- *How can I get the housework done and have fun at the same time?*
- *What can I do to laugh a lot today?*
- *How can I make today better than yesterday?*
- *How can I make my future more exciting than my past?*
- *How can I make myself a priority so I have more to give others?*
- *What do I love about myself?*
- *What am I grateful for?*
- *How can I honor my body today?*
- *What can I do to feel my emotions instead of eating them today?*
- *How can I become more connected to my internal joy?*
- *How can I make choices that benefit me, and everyone around me, at the same time?*
- *How can I live my best life?*

Exercise:

- Write down three of your own great questions to ask each day.

If you want great answers,
ask great questions.

Self-Care Tool #10
Choose to be Around People You Love

I used to spend a lot of time trying to get people to like me. In fact, the less they liked me, the more I tried to get them to like me. It was such a subtle activity I didn't realize I was doing it. I would say things I thought they wanted to hear. I would agree with their opinions and try to please and impress them with how I entertained, how I communicated, and how responsive I was to requests. I would actually put pressure on myself to abide by the actions I made up in my head about how they wanted me to act. The crazy part about it is that most of them would have liked me just fine even if I wasn't trying. More importantly, and actually quite shocking to me now, is I didn't consider whether or not I liked them. Honestly, I was so caught up in being liked that I never asked myself what my own opinion was. This was a very difficult pattern to break.

Somewhere along the line, I lost respect for my own opinion. Am I hungry? Do I like this food? Do I even like this person? What I realized is that I had many people in my life who liked me and I wasn't sure if I liked them. Isn't that strange? I had no idea if I liked certain people because I was so wrapped up in whether or not they liked me. I had to think about it when I spent time with them. I had to turn off my "try-to-be-pleasing act" and replace it with "am I having fun with this person?" Do I like spending my time with them? I cannot tell you how changing my focus in this area has changed my life.

I used to think this was an issue that only I had until I started coaching. I found many clients who, like me, spent time with people because they were liked by them. When I asked, "What do you like about them?" many times the response was a blank stare and the response, "They're okay, I guess." What happens is when we aren't giving ourselves enough love and approval, we are looking outside of ourselves to get it. When someone actually gives us some approval, we do whatever we can to keep getting it. We start doing an approval-earning dance based on what we think they like. This can become quite exhausting.

> *Change the question from:*
> *"Do they like me?"*
> *to "Do I like me?"*

I will share with you that one of my dominant, illogical, and negative belief systems is that if I get too successful or "big" in my life I will end up with no friends. I am not sure where this belief comes from, although I do have some ideas. The point is, it doesn't matter where the belief comes from, it only matters where it is taking me. What this belief was manifesting in my life was a desire to not do things that would cause me too much success. I would play down my success and my goals and my dreams to my friends because on some level, I believed that they wouldn't want to hang around.

In working with my coach/trainer, Martha Beck, I learned to turn this belief around to, "I must become big and be who I really am in order to see who my true friends are." My mantra is "Go big" in everything I try to do. This book was going to be a small e-book just for my clients, but now I am publishing it. To me, that feels very big and, yes, on some level I feel as if I might lose some friends. I just have to go after it to prove it wrong. Because the truth is, if someone is not happy for me because I'm following my dreams, that is not someone I want in my life.

What I have learned is that when we start truly loving and believing in ourselves, we don't hunt down these "likers" so much. We start thinking in terms of what *we* like and whom *we* like. We find people we adore and they adore us back. These are "our" people. There are no rules; it's just a great place to be. You suddenly have a built-in fan club of people you like.

Fill your life with people who will be excited for you when you lose weight—people who will applaud each and every accomplishment and still love you madly when you haven't accomplished anything that day. Make sure these are people you admire and respect and love. They should make you laugh and cry and genuinely feel alive. Don't settle for less; go and find your people.

Exercise:

- Make a list of people *you* love.

I don't need to search for people to love me, because I love me.
Now I just need to seek out people I love—and magically they seem to love me back.

Make Your Future Happen—
Don't Let It Happen to You

"You can design the future of your dreams."

Future Tool #1
Do Not Be Past-Focused

Often, I hear clients say that they want to get "back" to a weight they used to be. They want to weigh what they weighed in high school or before they had the baby. I always discourage this type of past-focused thinking. I like to have clients focus on the future and on a body they would like to have in one year or five years from now. Furthermore, that past body you had ended you up here, overweight again. It wasn't your permanent solution. This time, things can be different and this time can be the last time.

Many of us have pasts filled with pain and negative circumstances. Many of us feel we have had many failures—especially failed weight-loss attempts. When we define ourselves and our future abilities by these past attempts, we become discouraged and filled with regret. I like to look at my past as if it was perfect. It happened exactly as it was supposed to and there were no mistakes, just lessons and preparation. I don't see any reason to argue with my past or wish it was different. It is a waste of emotional energy. I choose to take that energy and focus on my future, something I feel I can have an impact on.

The truth is that you can't go back. The past is over. For some of us, this is a blessing. The good news, however, is that the future is yours for the taking. You can create a future that is better than your past. Many times, if you ask a past-focused person what their plans are for the future, they have no idea where they are going. They are being defined by who they used to be without taking control of who they want to be.

I can tell when someone I am working with is past-focused or defined by their past because they will say things like:

> That's just how I have always done it.
> That doesn't work for me; I have tried it.
> I've always had this issue my entire life.
> This is just how I am.
> I am not the kind of person who can do that.
> I've always been overweight; it's just me.
> I am not a very good athlete.

When I hear this kind of talk, I know the client is being defined by the "evidence" of their past, evidence that they have been unconsciously looking for in order to prove their terrible belief systems. Although I do believe we need to learn from our past and grow from the mistakes we have made, I never recommend that you define yourself by what you haven't been able to accomplish yet.

It's time to turn your head around and start focusing on the road ahead. The past is over and gone; you cannot go back there and change it or be younger again. Your past set you up to be the person you are today. Love it for what it did and say goodbye. It's time to get excited about your future.

Exercise:

- Name the ways in which you are past focused.
- What in your past do you focus on or let define you that is negative?

The past does not define who we are.

We do.

Future Tool #2
Top-Five Outcomes

One of the required exercises I do with all my clients is to have them write down the top-five outcomes they want in their life. In other words, what are the five most important things you want to have happen in your life before you pass away? It's shocking how many of us have never considered this question. I stump client after client with this question. After some prodding, we manage to get five outcomes on paper.

Here is a sample outcome list from one of my clients:

1. Have a deeper spiritual connection to myself and my Creator and maintain it daily.
2. Lose seventy pounds of fat and maintain my ideal weight the rest of my life without struggle.
3. Get a better job that is aligned with my values that pays me enough to save 1M for my early retirement.
4. Be an amazing mother to my four children by setting a great example and being available to them emotionally.
5. Have a hot, steamy, intimate relationship with my husband for the next fifty years.

After completing the outcome list, I have them describe what they did yesterday and how they spent their time. The above client's day looked like this:

> Woke up and got myself and kids ready for work and school.
> Dropped off kids at school.
> Ran errands.
> Worked eight hours at a job I dislike.
> Picked up kids.
> Made dinner.
> Cleaned house, did laundry.
> Helped kids with homework and put them to bed.
> Watched TV for a few hours with my husband.
> Went to sleep.
> (Overall feeling for the day was anxiety and exhaustion)

After the exercise, we then evaluate how much of their daily life is spent on things that contribute to their top-five outcomes. As you can see by this typical example above, very little of her time was consciously devoted to making sure she was working toward her dreams. It's usually a profound realization when we do this. Most of us don't spend anywhere near a proper proportion of time on things that are important to us.

For example, most people feel that one of their top outcomes is to have an amazing relationship with their spouse. When we look at how much time they spend on their relationship, the answer in is the negative numbers. In fact, most people spend the majority of time with their spouses doing daily agendas and arguing about trivial matters. Often, I will recommend setting up a date night to encourage time spent away from the kids and away from errands in order to fully engage with one another. At this suggestion, I hear, "Well we don't have time or money or energy to spend one day a week with each other." I remind them of how much they paid for their car, which didn't make the outcome list. I ask them how much time they spend watching TV or being on the Internet, again nowhere on the outcome list.

It is possible to invest in your relationship and be a busy, full-time working mom. I have been married for eight years and I can count on one hand the number of date nights we have missed. We have a standing appointment with a babysitter and we count on that time to reconnect and love each other. My husband is one of the most important things in my life and I don't just talk about it, I prove it by giving both of us one night a week. Our friends know not to call us on Tuesday because we won't be home or available for anything but each other. It is not negotiable.

I highly recommend you do something similar with each of your outcomes. Make sure your life is supporting what you want. It truly is a choice. I have seen client after client change their life and their level of satisfaction by having a guideline to follow. Try to spend time going after what you have thought about, not just committing to a daily grind that doesn't spark your soul.

Exercise:

- What are your top-five outcomes? Why?
- How much time do you currently spend on fulfilling these outcomes?
- Fill in the following worksheet.

If one of the most important things in your life is your health, one hour per day is a reasonable amount of time to spend on it.

TOP-FIVE OUTCOMES WORKSHEET

OUTCOME 1 _____
(e.g., Lose 50 pounds and live in a healthy, fit body by Jan 2007)

Why you want to achieve this?
(e.g., so I can focus on something else besides my weight and feel strong)

_____

_____

The obstacles to achieving this outcome are:
(e.g., overeating, burying my emotions, my negative beliefs about myself and abilities)

_____

_____

Strategies to overcome the obstacles are:
(e.g., read, understand and actually apply all the tools in this book that resonate with me; change my beliefs that aren't working and feel my emotions without fear of them ruining my life)

_____

_____

_____

OUTCOME 2 _____
Why you want to achieve this?

_____

_____

_____

The obstacles to achieving this outcome are:

_____

_____

Strategies to overcoming the obstacles are:

_____

_____

_____

_____

OUTCOME 3 _____
Why you want to achieve this?

_____

_____

The obstacles to achieving this outcome are:

_____

_____

_____

_____

Strategies to overcoming the obstacles are:

_____

_____

_____

_____

_____

OUTCOME 4 _____

Why you want to achieve this?

_____

_____

The obstacles to achieving this outcome are:

_____

_____

Strategies to overcoming the obstacles are:

_____

_____

_____

OUTCOME 5 _____

Why you want to achieve this?

_____

_____

I he obstacles to achieving this outcome are:

_____

_____

_____

Strategies to overcoming the obstacles are:

_____

_____

_____

Future Tool #3
What Do You Really Want?

Another exercise I do regularly with clients is to have them write a list of fifty things they want. For some reason, most clients cannot come up with fifty. It's strange that we don't think about what would make us happy on a regular basis. A much easier list to complete is what we *don't* want. Most of us spend a lifetime coming up with things we don't like. What do you really want? You might start the list with items you want to buy and vacations you want to take; you can put down little items and big items, big dreams, and little conveniences. Did you know you were yearning for these things?

I believe that what we genuinely want is very important information. I believe it is code for directions to our destiny. If we can figure out what we want and start doing what we want without being stifled by negative beliefs or negative feelings, we can find our way to where we are meant to be: where our work in the world is and where our highest level of joy resides. When we follow our heart, so to speak, our life becomes more truthful and more effortless. Our purpose starts to illuminate and the path we are meant to follow gets clearer.

The extent you don't know what it is you want is the extent you won't ever get it. Many times we are so busy surviving our daily, busy lives we don't stop to consider our dreams. We believe we will never be able to get what we want so we think daydreaming is frivolous. We have two kids and a mortgage after all. I assure you it is not frivolous; in fact, it is required. You are programmed to find your destiny, and if you pay attention, you will.

Getting what you want out of life is not tiring or exhausting, it is energizing. Many times, I hear that my clients can't go after what they want because they don't have any energy left. I tell them they are exhausted because they are swimming against their own current. They are tired of fighting themselves, ignoring their dreams, and participating in a life that doesn't feed their soul. Going after what you want will not deplete you; it will add more energy to your life than you knew you had.

Exercise:

- Make a list of twenty-five things you want. (Do not skip this one. List all twenty-five—do it now.)

Future Tool #4
You Have a Lot of Time Left

Think of your life as a horizontal straight line. At the beginning of the line, put a 0 to represent the day you were born. At the end of the line, put the number 100. Now, tick on the appropriate area in between these two numbers your age now. As you look at this diagram, see the space that represents the time you have already lived, then look at how much time you possibly have left to live.

I call this tool the future diagram to help you consider how much of your life you might have left. If you are planning on living until you are one hundred years old (which is not unrealistic when you consider the advances that will be made in science over the next twenty years), how many years do you have left to live? For some of you, you have more life to live than you have already lived. When you further consider that the first fifteen years of your life you were living according to the demands of school and the wishes of your parents, you have a much more self-defined life to live in your future than you might have already experienced.

When we are young, we are typically very future-focused; this makes our life exciting and compelling. We look forward to graduation, college, jobs, marriage, children, and then what—maybe retirement? It's at this point that many of us become past-focused. We start looking at where we have been instead of where we are going.

Now, you have the tools to really make something happen. You have been developing some important wisdom during your past so that you can now use it in your life to make things happen. Don't just look forward to retiring and sitting. Step up! Now is the time to plan and make some great outcomes happen. IT'S NEVER TOO LATE.

Where are you going?

This is a fantastic question to consider. Where will you be in five years if you keep living this way? Where will you be in ten, twenty, or thirty years? What exactly is it that you want to have many years down the road? Are you on the path you need to be on? What can you change to put yourself on the path to achieving what you most want from your life?

I love the imagery of the rudder on a boat. If you move it just slightly today, you will end up in a completely different location five years from now than if you just left it alone. It's not as if we have to make a massive change in our current lives to create the future we desire. If you are on your way to where you want to go, then congratulations and hold steady. But, if you want to be somewhere different in ten years, the time to change is now.

How much money do you want to have? Where do you want to be living? What kind of work do you want to do? How fit do you want to be? Lay your foundation. Go and get what you want.

One of my most memorable clients came to me when she was seventy years old wanting to lose some weight. After a very short amount of time, I realized that the reason she had gained the weight and was continuing to pack it on was because her life was stagnant. She was retired from her job and her dear husband had passed a few years earlier. With further inquiry, I was able to discover that she was literally waiting to die. She saw this "last chapter" of her life as a waiting game. She was a bystander, watching her kids live their lives, but she didn't feel as if she had one of her own. She talked a lot about the past and how great her life had been and how old she was now. When we did this exercise and explored the idea that she could have thirty more years to live, she was dumbfounded. I offered the idea that they could be the best thirty years of her life so far. This was a huge turning point for her. The thought of living the next thirty years lonely and overweight with no excitement or accomplishments seemed like a sentence. She kicked her life into gear. She quit drinking, lost all the weight, started exercising regularly, and got involved in activities that she truly enjoyed. She met a nice man to share her life with. She is an inspiration to any of us who think it is too late.

I love the concept that if we ran at full-focused speed our entire life, courageously seeking and fulfilling our dreams, we couldn't come close to fulfilling our potential. With belief in this truth, there is no time in our life that we can disregard as a time not to be growing or becoming. No matter how old or how busy we are, we have potential to tap and dreams to consider. At the end of our lives, we will not have fulfilled our full level of potential, but it would be nice to know we died trying.

Exercise:

- How old do you believe you will be when you die?
- How many years do you have left?
- How does this make you feel?

Tick where you are now.

0   **100**

You get to decide what you
will be like at
80 years old.
Happen to your life;
don't let it happen to you.

Future Tool #5
What Are You an Example Of?

When someone looks at your life, what would they say you are an example of? Think about the answer to this question. The good example you set and the bad example you set. See how you represent on this planet. What are you representing? Are you a follower, living by someone else's rules or desires? Are you an example of what happens when you choose to live as a victim? Or, are you an example of someone who is living the best life they know how, and with all their heart?

Are you someone who never quits? Someone who is always making something happen? What do you want your life to be? An example to your children and your friends? How about making your life an example of someone who got over the weight struggle and took that energy and created a life she loved? How about an example of someone who takes responsibility for herself and doesn't blame circumstances or anyone else for her current life?

I mentioned earlier in this book that my main questions are: *How can I be an example of what is possible?*

How can I defy the odds of what I think is possible? How can I help other people do the same? I truly want my life to show that if you set a goal with your heart, stick to it with courageous belief, and love yourself through the process, you can achieve it. I want other people to believe they can be free of the weight struggle because they see me as proof that it can be done. I want other women to go after their dreams because they watched me having fun going after mine. Ultimately, I want to show how much energy is freed up when you drop the weight obsession and how much power we have to use in contributing to the good in this world.

Wouldn't it be amazing if someone could look at you and be inspired? Not impressed by what you do, but inspired by who you are. Maybe someday someone can look at you and say, "If she can do it, maybe I can too." I see this as more than just a choice; it is a responsibility we have to represent our Creator.

Exercise:

• If someone were to use your life to illustrate a point—what would you be used as an example of?

Future Tool #6
Goals Are Not Just for Executives and Business Plans

We have all heard how powerful goal-setting is, but many of us don't think our goals are grand enough to write down. We think our desires are simple and not impressive, so why write them down? Well, I say if you want any of those goals to happen, you have a much better chance of success if you write them down. The reason I believe this to be true is by writing them down, we are taking them from the dream world and creating a place where they exist in the world and not just in our minds. There is something about the act of writing them down that makes them exist in a way they haven't existed before; it makes them important enough to be acknowledged.

Writing down goals develops the "planning" muscle, which is one of the most important muscles in weight loss. It is good practice in planning your life instead of just wating for it to happen. The more my clients plan the details of their lives, the more weight they lose— period. I have seen it time and time again. Committing to the daily goals of exercising and eating in a well-planned, thought-out way seems to get them halfway to accomplishing it. By building the practice of seeing themselves achieve their smaller daily goals, they become convinced they will be able to achieve the bigger ones as well. Success truly does breed success. With goals written and scheduled, you won't be looking up one day and saying, "Where did the time go?" Instead, you will know exactly what you are doing with your time and it will lead you to accomplishing all your goals.

I highly recommend writing goals on paper on a regular basis and not just once a year. Start with your top-five outcomes and write a twenty-five-year goal for each outcome. Then, break it down to ten-, five-, and one-year, and eventually, into ninety-day goals. Based on your ninety-day goals, pull out your calendar and make a daily action plan for all the action items required to achieve the goals. Then, every quarter, look at your goals and your accomplishments. Celebrate your successes and set some new ones. Before you know it, a year will have gone by and your goal will be accomplished. The year is going to pass anyway—you might as well reap some specific rewards from it. I love the quote, "A year from now, you will wish you had started today." Start right now, your future self will thank you for it.

Here is an example of one of my outcomes with more specific goals:

Outcome: To be at my natural weight, free from a struggle with food and to be energetic, active, and strong.

25-Year Goal: To hike a mountain with my son and keep up with him even though he will be a young athlete and I will be an "older" lady.

10-Year Goal: To be an expert skier, an advanced water-skier, and to have hiked the Grand Canyon.

5-Year Goal: To be able to keep up with my young sons in any sport they play. To always be in the game and not just on the sidelines.

1-Year Goal: To continue weightlifting regularly and walking at least four days a week. To be taking a yoga class regularly with a teacher who inspires me.

90-Day Goal: Research yoga teachers and take at least one class per week until I find a class I love. Continue with my regular workout routine that I already love.

For each of the listed goals, I further write a list of all the specific actions I will take and I have a deadline for each one. I actually have them documented on my calendar as important meetings that I try not to reschedule for any reason.

The important thing about goals is you must believe you can accomplish them. This is very different than hoping you will achieve them. There is a sense of certainty that must come from deep within you. When my clients tell me their goals, I ask them a series of questions about each one:

1. Do you think you can accomplish this?
2. Are you certain you will?
3. If your life depended on it, could you?
4. What are you willing to do or not do to make this goal happen?
5. What would you do differently if you were offered 500k to accomplish this goal on time?
6. What are the major obstacles that could prevent you from achieving this goal and what is your plan for over coming them?

Exercise:

Write down your goal: _____

_____

Now, answer these six questions.

1. Do you think you can accomplish this?

_____

_____

_____

2. Are you certain you will?

_____

_____

_____

3. If your life depended on it, could you?

_____

_____

4. What are you willing to do or not do to make this goal happen?

_____

_____

_____

5. What would you do differently if you were offered 500k to accomplish this goal on time?

_____

_____

_____

_____

_____

_____

_____

_____

6. What are the major obstacles that could prevent you from achieving this goal and what is your plan for overcoming them?

Obstacles:

_____

_____

_____

_____

_____

Your plan for overcoming them:

_____

_____

_____

_____

_____

_____

_____

Future Tool #7
Excuses

"But." Oh, the amount of times I've heard this one. "I would love to live the life of my dreams, but"... I don't want to hear it. The excuse is never good enough for me and it shouldn't be for you either.

I have my clients put all their excuses on paper. I encourage them to make a collection, then I remind them that excuses belong on paper and not in their lives. Excuses are rotten little dream-stealers. We believe in excuses at the expense of a life we would otherwise love.

I encourage you to write down all the excuses you have for not pursuing the life and the body you deserve. Many of these excuses you will see as legitimate and unchangeable—your lot in life, so to speak. I assure you, no excuse is worth the cost of a dream.

The best way to evaluate your excuses to see if they are reasons why you are doing something, versus an excuse for why you don't accomplish something, is to see how you feel about it. An excuse is disappointing and not true when it comes to who you really are. It is a reason you wish you hadn't used. It causes pain and disappointment.

A reason not to do something is not an excuse when you feel good or even stronger for believing it. For example, if you don't do the dishes because you went to work out and you feel good about this decision, then it is not an excuse as to why you didn't do the dishes; it is the reason you didn't do them and you stand by that reason and feel good about it. If, on the other hand, you didn't work out because you had dishes to do and you are disappointed by the choice you made, then it is an excuse as to why you didn't work out. You are disappointed because, to you, working out was more important than doing the dishes and it shouldn't have been used as an excuse.

Sometimes, I push my clients hard and shake them up when they are used to living with excuses. I get all over them and tell them their reasons are not good enough to pass the excuse test and they need to remove them from their lives. If they don't feel good about the choice, they shouldn't make it. I tell them they can have the excuses, they can write them down and even say them aloud, but they are strongly advised not to obey them unless they genuinely want to.

This simple act of writing down excuses has been an enlightening tool in many of my clients' lives. Many of their reasons seem illogical and ridiculous when written in ink. I had a client who said she couldn't eat fuel food because her cafeteria didn't offer good choices. I told her that I didn't think people credited their work cafeteria for their fabulous figure and she might have to bring her lunch to work. It was an astounding idea to her; so shockingly, she hadn't considered it. She told me she didn't have enough time to make her lunch because her life was already so busy. I told her that I thought it was a lame excuse, not to mention a terrible belief that wasn't true. She agreed once she saw it written down on her list, started making her lunch, and immediately lost three pounds in five days! What excuses do you have that you don't realize you have? Think about them and write them down now.

> *Excuses are really*
> *little white lies*
> *disguised as reality.*

Read the list, then go get your shoes on and take a walk. Eat the very next time you get hungry and stop when you are full. Look at your excuse list regularly, then state, "Your opinion is noted, but I disagree." Then, go about living a life that makes you proud... and excuse-free! Believe in yourself, not your excuses.

You can't keep living the same life, doing the same things, and expect the results to be different. You have to change your life to change the result. If you want your body to look completely different, your daily life will have to look completely different by eliminating some, if not all, of your current excuses.

Exercise:

- List your five top excuses.
- What does it feel like to read this list?

---

*Excuses belong on paper,
not in your life.*

Future Tool #8
You Must Keep Moving Forward Because There Is No Going Back

Many of us who have weight issues are all-or-nothing thinkers. We go on a diet, then blow it and give up on the whole thing. We start exercising and miss a day, then we return to how we used to be. This is the only difference between those who succeed and those who fail. Those who succeed just keep moving forward. They keep going toward their goal NO MATTER WHAT.

Every time you make a mistake and keep moving forward toward your goal anyway, you become stronger. Anytime an unexpected obstacle gets in your way, you have an opportunity to grow. You overeat at one meal, the very next meal you get back on track without judgment or anxiety. You will not win every single time. This is not about being perfect or doing it just right, this is about progress and moving forward.

I love to use the mountain metaphor when talking about the journey to weight loss. We all start at the bottom of the mountain and see it looming up before us. It seems daunting and difficult. If we continue to take one step at a time each day, we will be at the top of that mountain before we realize it, and the view is wonderful. On this climb, we will fall down. We will trip. We will lose our balance and tumble sometimes. This is not a reason to run all the way down the mountain to the bottom and say that the climb did not work. This is time to get back up, keep our eye on the top, and start stepping again. Many things will come to the edge of the path and tempt you to veer off in another direction or take a break for a week, or year, to catch your breath. You just put up your hand, say, "Your opinion is noted." And keep climbing. No matter what the scale says. No matter what your mother says. No matter what mistakes you have made or how slow your progress is, just keep moving forward. If you keep moving, you will get closer every day.

It is not necessarily a bad thing when you have a slip-up in your plan. I actually like it when a client screws up their plan. I always see it as an opportunity to learn something and create a new tool for them. If they missed a day of walking, I ask them what was going on. I do not scold them, nor do I allow them to scold themselves. We evaluate what might have caused it. When they try to say, "I just didn't feel like it," I always probe—"Well why not? What, specifically, were you feeling? What was going on?" Many times, we find something that the client wasn't aware of. We learn something new and now we can make a plan to deal with it or change the belief system. Because of the slip-up, we are further along than we would have been.

Sometimes, it will feel like you are leaping and other times it will feel like you are just inching along. As long as you are moving forward, you will get there eventually. The alternative is to give up and not get there at all! This is not a good alternative. It will come. When you get there, you will be glad you kept moving and trusted in yourself to make it.

We want to lose weight right now because we have been sold a story of instant results. There is nothing instant about losing weight. If you find yourself wanting to be thin now, you must realize that what you really want is to feel good now. You believe that thinness will make you feel better. It's *you* who will make *you* feel better.

The emotional process of getting to a place where you don't overeat is a reward in and of itself. It creates freedom that lasts for the rest of your life if you do it thoroughly. Being thorough means you stop and pay attention to your setbacks to learn from them and remove them as issues in your life. You must build your emotional foundation so you feel strong and lean, not just physically, but emotionally as well.

Setting the goal is not just about achieving the goal; it is about building the strength that is required to achieve it. It is a great view from the top of the mountain and that is a nice prize, but the feeling of accomplishment and strength is the real prize. You can use that strength and believe in yourself to climb your next mountain. You can see how much you have to look forward to.

I have many mountains I want to climb. Each one of my outcomes and goals fuels me to keep climbing and challenging myself and getting to know myself more intimately. I get excited about the process. For example, the thought of hiking with my young-adult son when I am many years older creates a compelling future when I can imagine us talking about our lives and enjoying the beauty of nature together. I love that idea. It makes me want to work out right now to keep myself fit for the time when I will be hiking with him, instead of watching him live his life from a rocking chair!

> When you have a choice between being a spectator or a player, choose player every time.

Most clients I work with who are over forty pounds overweight are stagnant. They don't have a compelling future that is driving them. They are not thinking about where they will be in ten years. They haven't created a beautiful mountain to climb or a dream to look forward to. Mostly, they are hanging out at the bottom of many prospective mountains, thinking about what they are going to eat and what diet they can go on after the holidays. They feel defeated before they have even started.

There is nothing about a crash diet that inspires your soul. There is nothing about being thin that compels you spiritually unless it comes with self-growth and renewal. We all want to have exciting and wonderful lives. When we sit and watch life pass us by, we become stagnant. We wait for our life to happen and many of us are very disappointed with what it brings.

We are waiting to see what rolls down the mountain instead of climbing up to get what we really want. It is a cycle of wanting and never achieving that makes our lives stagnant and makes us sometimes feel hopeless.

Stagnant lives are fertile soil for fat to grow. You can be very busy and stagnant, so don't confuse activity for progress toward your dreams. Imagine yourself at the bottom of the mountain, running in circles. No progress, just activity. This is not how you accomplish your dreams, and all the true desires ignored breed discontentment and fat. Look up. Start stepping!

Exercise:

• When you stumble...and you will....what is your plan to keep moving forward when you would rather give up?

> *Stop looking for the magic pill.*
> *You are the magic.*

Future Tool # 9
Have Your Future Self Be Your Mentor

Once you become future-focused, you can start visualizing your future self. Your future self is already at the top of the mountain; she is at her natural weight and she is, undoubtedly, more accomplished than you are now. She is you, just further along the path. She is who you are without the fat, without the struggle, with a sense of peace and fulfillment and accomplishment. She is who you already are without the negative belief systems that hold you back.

One of the best tools I use on a daily basis is to use my future self as a mentor. She is my ticket to the life I want. I am always asking myself what my future self would do in certain situations. I imagine her free from the negative belief systems I currently have. She has the confidence of completion that I can borrow when I am feeling anything but confident. She is at the top, with a clear view, telling me of what to be careful and of what I need to steer clear. She shows me that achievement is possible. By believing in her, I believe in myself.

As a mentor now, I would love to have been able to give my past self some advice. I am her future self and

I would go back and tell her not to worry so much. I would tell her how loved she was. I would tell her that I was proud of her for surviving her loneliness and desperation. I would remind her to keep working hard and to trust herself and follow her intuition. I would tell her that the view is beautiful and worth every step and obstacle along the way.

For some of you, this might seem a little strange and uncomfortable. Talking to yourself and accessing your own wisdom may be foreign to you. I promise you this is a skill worth developing. All the guidance you will ever need is within you now. You can lead yourself to the right books and the right people to help you along your journey, but no one else has all the answers for you. It doesn't matter if you hire the best coach in the universe; they will only be able to guide you to yourself for your own answers. There is no coach that knows your dreams and the path you need to follow to achieve them. You are your own coach, your own guide, and your own wisdom; you and the infinite wisdom that flows through you at this very moment.

See yourself at the bottom, at the top, and in between. See yourself at your current weight and your ideal weight. Visualize the journey. Visualize the entire process of losing the weight. You need to anticipate the times when you will struggle and plan for them. You need to think about the times when your weight loss will plateau and have a plan for how to handle the evitable struggle that you'll have and recognize having the desire to give up. If you can come to expect that this will happen, you won't be so caught off-guard and willing to throw in the towel if it happens.

I find it helpful to have my clients write out a story of how they think it will happen. You can try this technique as well. Write the journey before it actually happens. Include all the ups and downs. Anticipate people complimenting you on your weight loss. Anticipate the first time you put on a size ten or the first time the scale reads 167 when it read 165 the day before. What will that feel like? How will you handle it? Anticipate feeling fearful and wanting to sabotage your success in favor of a belief system that didn't work. See yourself facing a stressful situation in your life and wanting to give up on your dreams because you can't handle it. See your future self, peaceful and supportive and knowing, as if she realizes each setback is a perfect part of this process.

I promise you will be challenged. You may get sick or injured. Your husband might leave you or a friend might die. How will you remain connected to yourself? How will you stay committed to your dreams when you find such a good reason to give it up and just survive? You will do it by looking up and seeing your future self. You will do it by knowing, in the deepest sense, who you are and that no matter what happens, you can and will have what it is you truly desire. This is when your strength will be tested and increased. This is when you can set an example and become more of who you really are. Plan for greatness despite the circumstances and you will find it.

Exercise:

- Describe your future self five years from now in detail.
- What advice would you (now) tell your past self?
- What guidance does your future self tell you now?

> *Don't expect it to be easy.*
> *Expect it to be hard, and*
> *know you can handle it.*

Don't Ever, Ever, Ever Give up!

"Do or do not—there is no try." Yoda

*I*n my chosen profession, there are two schools of thought. On one side of the spectrum, people talk a lot about giving up on dieting and accepting themselves at any weight. They teach you to eat what you want, when you want, without direct regard to nutrition or exercise. The focus is mainly on loving and accepting yourself at any weight, without much emphasis on losing it. On the other side of the spectrum, there are those who say we should lose weight at any cost. They teach us that we should avoid parties and not eat any junk food or have any treats in our homes. These teachers teach that being fit is the way you can be healthy and happy without much regard for the emotional components and obstacles. This is where gastric bypass, obsessive exercising, and severe dieting can get completely out of control and cause much emotional damage for the sake of being "physically healthy."

I am right in the middle of both of these ideas. I believe we must accept ourselves and love ourselves; we must stop judging our bodies so harshly. I don't believe we have to accept being fat. Being overweight means we are eating too much and there is usually a painful emotional reason for this. I feel that if we can discover the reasons why we eat, we can change our habits and live our lives in a happy and comfortable way. We can understand on a deep fundamental level that weight isn't really the issue and eating really isn't the issue. We find that when we are happy and in line with our own guidance, we have no need to use food as an emotional tool. We have a tool belt filled with better ways to grow.

I also believe that taking care of ourselves physically is our way of loving ourselves and our bodies. Connecting with the physical body and using emotional tools to cope, instead of using food, are steps toward a peaceful kind of wholeness. I believe eating fuel that truly feeds our body and exercising in a way that promotes health are essential. I believe that we can have a body we are comfortable in and a life that is free from obsession with food and weight. I also think we can live in the world and have a piece of cake and go to a party that has food without panicking.

> *Loving your body now, as it is, and wanting it to be fit and thin do not have to be mututally exclusive.*

Our bodies and the way we carry them are a reflection of our inner life and our beliefs about who we are and what we deserve. I don't believe we have to be as thin as a movie star to be happy. I do believe that when we eat according to our body's wisdom and not in order to cope with our lives, we will arrive at a natural weight that works for us. This will be the weight we are comfortable with and doesn't take too much effort to maintain.

When I first lost weight, I got down to about a size six. I was very thin and was working out hard. I liked being a size six because jeans looked great and I could wear a bikini very comfortably. It turned out it was just too much work. I had to think about it too carefully and it didn't come naturally. I finally settled into a size eight with a level of exercise and eating that is practical for me. That's where my body stays when I listen to it and feed it and take care of it. This cooperation with my body frees me up to be comfortable in the world and to use my energy on something more productive than trying to look like a magazine cover.

This book is about finding *your* effortless weight. It is the place where you don't struggle; you feel strong, capable, and free. You feel healthy and natural and balanced. It has to do with who you are from the inside out. There is no doubt in my mind that this is what true beauty can mean for each of us. We might not end up looking like an airbrushed model, but we feel so good physically and emotionally, we just don't care.

Use every tool in this book as much as you can. Again, the difference between those of you who will use this book and make a change and those of you who won't comes down to *applied knowledge*. I have read many books that have taught me so much about life. When I actually did what the books told me to do, I changed my life. These tools were only effective when I applied them, not just understood them.

So, now you have the knowledge and many tools to make a difference in your life. If you sit back and say that you are different and that it won't work for you, simply go back to the chapter on belief systems and turn it around. If you are feeling tired and unable to take action, go to the chapter on feelings and make your life about what you want to do and not just what you feel like doing in the moment.

Each time you ignore your body or treat yourself in an unloving way, you are missing an opportunity to live at your highest level. You and I have every opportunity to make our lives better and our bodies thinner if we choose to take care in each moment.

There is no reason to stay overweight or be unhappy. Never settle with where you are if you aren't happy. I always tell my clients that we are not on the planet to be happy and thin. We are on the planet to give to ourselves first, then to the rest of the world. Your life can be an example of what is possible. You can shine. Now is your moment; let *you* be the one who has decided that this time, it will be permanent.

Lay down your weapon and make peace with your body. There is too much war and too much fighting within our own lives. We work against ourselves as if our body is the enemy and we have to trick it and deprive it and control it. It is not unlike war. Using force instead of peace will not give us the permanent solutions we are looking for. When we work with our own body and use our own wisdom, there is no enemy to fight anymore. There is nothing to struggle against and we can find peaceful ways to get what our body wants (fuel) and what we want (freedom from the struggle).

Let's end this battle within us and work on ending the war we are participating in. Let's take all the collective energy that we women have been using to lose weight and obsess over our bodies and use it for something more productive. Let's work with ourselves and support each other in finding a way that speaks to our hearts and souls. Let's use our weight as a way to get to know ourselves intimately, and let's work with it as a training ground for emotional strength. Let's work hard to find the reason we are eating more than our body requires for fuel and take action so we can stop it. Let's arrive at our natural weight by unraveling the cause, not by fighting the symptom. Think about what we could do with the billions of dollars, the hours of time, and the mental energy we have collectively used on the symptom. Think about what we could do in the world.

Now, go, get it done.

Food and thinness are
cheap substitutes for real joy.
May you find your real joy
and share it with the world....

I would love to hear from you.
Please email me your thoughts or your questions
to brooke@futuresunlimitedcoaching.com.

If you want some coaching...

If, after reading this book, you are interested in additional coaching, please call 1-877-817-1680 or visit Brooke's website at www.futuresunlimited-coaching.com. There, she offers the following:

1. **Why Can't I Lose Weight Audiobook**

2. **Coach in a Box**. Includes eight CDs, a workbook, a food journal, a feelings/beliefs journal, and a list of all the tools given to one-on-one clients.

3. **Quarterly Seminars and Workshops**

4. **Specialized year-long programs** for exclusive groups of ten. These accepted individuals meet in person with Brooke for a year of intensive group and one-on-one coaching. On alternating months, the group meets in person and daily online through messaging and email. This is a group for serious clients who are ready to invest in ending the struggle permanently.

5. **Monthly email coaching with Brooke**

About the Author

Brooke Castillo has been studying weight loss for over fifteen years. She has used her degree in psychology from Santa Clara University, her own experience in losing over seventy pounds, and her natural affinity for helping others, to put together a weight-loss program with proven results. She presents a program based on managing emotions, belief systems, and unhealthy habits that contribute to overeating. Those willing to commit themselves to a program of self-reflection, goal planning, and overcoming unwelcome internal thinking are destined to achieve their goal of successful weight loss without actually dieting.

Brooke has a thriving coaching practice where she has worked one-on-one with individuals committed to her weight-loss ideas. She is a certified North Star Coach, trained personally by Dr. Martha Beck and her associates. Because of the popularity of her work, she offers seminars and online packages to address the needs of others who want to lose weight. Her year-long intensive program, in particular, has been a huge success.

Brooke, her husband, and her two children live in Shingle Springs, CA.